Get Real!

Building Knowledge & Wealth Through Real Estate

Get Real!

Building Knowledge & Wealth Through Real Estate

By

Matthew Harms

Get Real!: Building Knowledge Wealth Through Real Estate © 2023 by Matthew Harms & Penforhire, Inc.

ISBN: 979-8-9893005-0-1

First edition: 2023

For every bank that has taken a chance in financing our efforts at making the real estate world a better place.

For every amazing real estate professional out there doing their best to serve their clients with ethics and compassion in an industry often too focused on profits and get-rich-quick schemes.

For every client, whether buyer, seller, or property manager, who has trusted us with one of the largest and most important decisions of their lives.

And most of all, for everyone who has continued to believe in me, no matter how implausible the aspiration may have been. You are the reason books like this continue to be written.

Table of Contents

Introduction

At one point or another, we have all struck up a conversation with someone at a family or work event we've never met before. There is generally a list of small-talk questions we roll through like, "How do you know so-and-so?," "Where are you from?," and "What do you do for a living?"

Then they say, "I'm in real estate."

The response of "in real estate" is cryptic and for no good reason. What does that even mean? Literally thousands of jobs could all fall under the real estate umbrella: brokers, agents, appraisers, investors, etc. I'm not here to bore you with the extensive list – I promise – but, we will speak about several of these roles throughout the book as they relate to different concepts and strategies for making an actual living in real estate.

When you ask a doctor what they do, they will generally reply with what they specialize in, rather than leave the conversation at, "I'm in medicine." Maybe this is the reason there seems to be an allure surrounding the thought of getting into real estate as well. It could also be the reality television shows hyping up the glamor of selling million-dollar homes to celebrities, making a fortune by buying run-down homes and flipping them for significant profits, or what appears to be a laid-back career choice where you can live life on your terms with passive income coming in every month. Well, if any of those are the reasons you picked up this book and may be thinking of getting into real estate, it might be time to think again.

Spoiler alert: Less than 5% of licensed real estate agents make more than 95% of commissions generated from real estate transactions. A large portion of real estate agents do not even make enough money to call it a career, and some never make a single dollar. The same can be said for investors who buy rental properties and show off on social media with all their techniques and strategies for helping to make you just as successful as they are. Most people wind up becoming a landlord and hate it, never realizing how much work is actually involved in what they thought was supposed to be a passive income stream. A large majority of would-be flippers lose money on their first project and are done with real estate for good.

But there is good news for some of you, and that is the validation that more generational wealth can be created in the real estate industry than any other. Whether you decide to get a real estate license or not, anyone can buy or sell a property, find deals, or employ other creative strategies to build wealth. In most states, getting a license is a very low barrier to entry that will only cost you a few hundred dollars and around 50-100 hours of your time, but just having a license does not guarantee success. There are plenty of starving real estate agents nationwide, and an equal number of folks making millions without a license – sometimes without a college or high school diploma. The trick is figuring out what you want to do and then having the discipline to pursue it.

No one is going to chase after you in real estate to make sure you are doing what needs to get done. As an agent, buyers and sellers will not come looking for you just because you passed your test last week. As an investor, deals are not just going to show up on your doorstep, and the funds to close the deals you do manage to find will not magically appear in your bank account. The belief of real estate being easy money is one many people have lost their shirts by subscribing to. No doubt there is the *potential* to make good money in real estate, but the same could be said for professional sports. Just because you bought a baseball bat doesn't mean you have the chance of becoming the next Babe Ruth.

I've been around the "real estate" market in one capacity or another for the last twenty-plus years. During that time, I have seen my share of *stuff,* to put it mildly. Back in the early 2000s, when mortgages that did not require any proof of income were getting handed out like drugs at a rave and banks truly let you purchase a home with no money down, I had big plans of becoming a tycoon straight out of college.

Get Real!

How difficult could it be? My partner (more like best friend and sidekick, who knew as little as I did) and I set our sights on a popular college town in upstate New York where we planned on buying as many multi-family homes or stately Victorians that could be converted into student housing. We would then sit back and collect the inflated rents we were sure the parents would pay to keep their kids out of the dorms.

Within weeks of starting our search, we had multiple prospects lined up. The cash flow projections looked good, a local realtor assured us he could get the sellers to work with us on price and terms, and his office had expertise in the student rental market. The next thing I knew, we were sitting across the closing table, writing checks for some ancillary closing fees, signing our lives away, and walking out with keys to the first three properties in what we thought would become our empire. Yep, you read that right. Two twenty-something-year-olds managed to buy more real estate over the course of a few weeks than some grown adults amass in their entire lives. Heck, my parents never even owned property, and I was still living with them in a rented two-bedroom apartment at the time.

I was on top of the world, and we stayed on top of the world…for the first few weeks anyway. Then, the cracks started to show. No, not actual cracks in the foundation, although those might have been easier to handle than the reality of our situation. Once rent payments were due, payments were nowhere to be found. It felt unfathomable since we made it a condition at closing that we would not buy the properties vacant. We did not want to carry the expenses each month while trying to find tenants, and neither one of us had a substantial amount of reserves to cover us if the process went on for longer than expected. Come on, we weren't stupid after all. Or were we?

Turns out, the realtor we worked with represented both us and the sellers. There is nothing wrong with that in and of itself, but apparently, the sellers were also agents on his team. He also happened to own the mortgage company that was so eager to give us 106% financing. They even found us all of the tenants for the three buildings, at no cost. What we viewed as exceptional customer service turned out to be anything but. The only thing worse than a vacant unit is a unit occupied by bad tenants, especially in a tenant-friendly state. Since these tenants would ultimately become our problem, the realtor focused solely on filling vacancies without screening or appropriately qualifying them.

We made so many mistakes back then it is painful and honestly difficult even to remember each of them. From investing in an area too far away for us to easily get to the properties if needed, to trusting others too much, to the ultimate kicker of not having any backup plans – we were in way over our heads, and everyone knew it except us. We did our best for a few months, driving up there on a regular basis to collect what little rent we could, working overtime at our day jobs to cover the money we were hemorrhaging, and even trying to sell the properties back to the original sellers at a loss. When phone calls from the local police department started coming in about drug raids and doors being knocked down by battering rams, we had had enough.

You might be wondering why in the world you should listen to anything I have to say, unless, of course, you are just looking for a book full of cringe-worthy stories. In either case, you are in luck. After letting the bank foreclose on those three properties and suffering years' worth of setbacks due to destroyed credit scores, battered confidence, and the stigma that comes with defaulting on a loan, I have learned significantly from those mistakes and compiled plenty of other stories where we were no longer the butt of the jokes.

Today, I run my own real estate brokerage company in three states. We have helped numerous people buy and sell millions of dollars worth of real estate and achieve their wildest dreams. Along with two other partners (the real kind), we operate an investment company that currently owns and manages over sixty rental units and flips a few houses every year. Despite being licensed in such a large footprint, all our investments are located in the same few zip codes where we know the market like the back of our hands. The pitfalls I fell victim to all those years ago may not exist in the same way under today's stricter lending guidelines, but the lessons learned were timeless. We started with nothing four years ago and now own over four million dollars worth of property, producing an annual net income of close to two hundred thousand dollars.

Whether you just want to learn just enough about real estate to help buy your first home, are looking to start a career as a real estate agent, or are looking to make the big money all these influencers and television personalities tell you is possible (after buying their course), this book can help you hit the ground running. But be warned up front, you must be open-minded and hardworking. There is no magic secret anyone can tell you for becoming an overnight success in real estate, and if anyone tells you otherwise – run! Needless to say, there will be a colorful story here and there to go along with the lessons. If you can't have fun with this, then it will eat you alive.

My only ask is this: be cautiously optimistic. Real estate is not rocket science. If I can do it, anyone can. While there will be strategies discussed for acquiring property with little to no money down and lending options for people with less than stellar credit, having capital and credit will make it easier to get started and grow faster. But with the right amount of creativity, there is no gap we cannot bridge. There will always be deals out there if you know where to look, so letting a few potentially good deals go by to avoid getting bogged down in a bad deal is a normal part of the learning curve.

Unfortunately, real estate lingo can be very confusing and heavy on the acronyms. Some investors use different terms interchangeably, while others speak in the three-letter language you will quickly pick up. For ease of reading, every time an industry-specific term is introduced, it will be defined in detail and made available in the glossary at the back of the book. All future uses of the word will be in the simplest form, generally, the acronym equivalent, to avoid bogging you down. If at any point you forget what a term means, feel free to flip back to the glossary for a refresher and then keep reading.

This book will predominantly focus on residential real estate. Many people have made plenty of money in commercial and industrial real estate, but at the time of writing this, those are not areas we have explored to any significant degree. I would not consider myself knowledgeable enough to offer any insights or advice on those segments and will not attempt to make it appear I can for the sake of selling a book. If you are passionate about learning more about those options and have little interest in residential real estate, then please have realistic expectations about the topics we will cover. However, if there is even a small part of you that has always wanted to know more about how to make money in the residential market or just get better at buying or selling your first or next home, then it's time to get real!

"If you think hiring a professional is expensive, wait till you hire an amateur."

— Red Adair

Chapter 1: Dream Team

I cannot stress enough how real estate is a team effort. Yes, one person may be able to handle all the moving pieces in a transaction on their own, but it is not practical since you are unlikely to be as great in law or finance as you are in construction or accounting. If, by some chance, you managed to handle every single aspect on your own, the time and opportunity cost would be tremendous. When there is an expert responsible for every facet of the transaction, not only are you ensured the highest quality of work, but you benefit from the leverage of time. This gives you the ability to go out in search of your next deal without being bogged down in the current one.

The key is to not just do random Google searches to build your network of dream team professionals. A bad partner can make a deal more painful than no partner at all. If you have been in real estate for a while, then you know exactly what I am talking about. Surround yourself with other people who are engaging in the types of real estate activities you want to participate in and pick their brains about who they work with and why. Use professional resource websites, Google reviews, Yelp reviews – you name it, use it. The more due diligence you put into vetting the right partners, the more time and money you will ultimately save in the long run.

The list of professionals and associates covered this chapter are in no particular order of importance. For anyone just beginning their real estate career without a deal already lined up and ready to go, you can start by adding anyone to your database of contacts. If you are more seasoned or close to making an offer on your first property, then I would highly advise starting with a lender first, since they are the ones who will give the seller confidence in your ability to get the deal done. Beyond that, realtors and inspectors should be crucial in making sure the first deal goes according to plan. Take this list and apply it to what you need most in your business right now.

Realtor

In almost all aspects of real estate, you will want a solid realtor on your dream team, if not several. Realtors are licensed professionals who specialize in helping home buyers and sellers in a variety of ways we will learn about throughout the book, but most importantly, they act as a mediator on potential deals. Of all the investment property we have acquired over the years, both rentals and flips, about half of them were listed on the Multiple Listing Service (MLS), which is the platform of choice for realtors nationwide. Because of this, we were able to forge relationships with those realtors and give them more insight into what we like and how we like to do business. Those relationships have proved invaluable over the course of the last year.

In one instance, a realtor was called in by a homeowner for a listing presentation, which is where the realtor estimates the value of the home and walks the seller through all the steps they will take to help them sell. The realtor took one step inside and realized they were going to have a very hard time selling the home. The best price it could get listed for would result in a paltry commission for the amount of work involved since the house could have been a contender for the show *Hoarders.* Each room was filled from floor to ceiling with boxes and other assorted junk to the point you could not enter, let alone walk. Even the grass outside was barely visible due to all the junk they had accumulated over the years. Knowing we specialize in situations like this, the realtor had the homeowner contact us. We negotiated a price, paid the realtor a generous referral fee for the lead, and proceeded to fill multiple dumpsters' worth of garbage so we could renovate, rent, and refinance!

A similar story happened on another deal that was already listed with a realtor. The price point was higher than we would usually pay, so the listing never popped up on our radar. We had done several deals with another agent in that office who saw the potential, and he knew the seller was extremely motivated and decided to present it to us with the lure of seller financing (which we will discuss in the next chapter). In this situation, the realtor had her own financial interest in mind, knowing that if we liked the deal, she would now become our agent on the buying side and collect a commission – which is okay. Thanks to her phone call, we were able to acquire a property $200K under market value without paying a penny out of our own pockets.

These are the reasons you want to have realtors in your network, but be sure to keep in mind this relationship is a two-way street. If you are flipping a home, there are two options when listing it for sale. If you go the For Sale By Owner (FSBO) road, you will save money on the commission, but you need to ask yourself where that deal came from in the first place. If a realtor helped you acquire the property, it would be foolish not to use them for the sale. The few thousand dollars you will pay out in commission goes a long way to show you are loyal to them, and it will motivate them to find you more deals. Being greedy never pays in the long run. The same goes for a rental property. When you need to fill vacancies, go back to the realtor who sold you the property.

Contractors

Contractors are the next group of people you will want on your dream team, and yes, that is intentionally plural. Even if you know a fantastic contractor who you think will do most of the work for you, it is always good to have at least three at your disposal. This is critically important in some geographic areas where skilled or motivated labor is difficult to find, as it is in our main areas of operation. There is only so much work one person or company can take on at a time, and you have no way of knowing if you are getting the best price without getting multiple bids. The longer your renovations get delayed or the higher over budget they wind up costing can quickly become the most significant impact on whether you make money or not, regardless if that comes in the form of lost rent on a cashflow property or additional holding costs on a flip.

This is a good point to draw a distinction between a contractor and a handyman. While having a handyman, someone capable of performing a wide range of small duties, is crucial in keeping projects running smoothly and preventing larger issues down the road often caused by neglect, they are no substitute for a licensed and insured contractor. For any work where a permit is required, a handyman will not qualify. For any property you intend to sell remodeled at a profit, the new owners are likely going to want to know what warranties, if any, are coming with the work. Most reputable contractors have varying warranties on the work they perform, which are transferable on sale. Even if you are not planning to sell, it is nice to have the peace of mind of knowing the person you just gave a substantial deposit for work not yet performed is not likely to run off without completing the job, which unfortunately happens more often than I would like to admit in this business.

Whether you have one contractor or five, it is also helpful to have skilled laborers who specialize in trades like electrical, plumbing, and HVAC. Oftentimes, the general contractor will have these specialists at their disposal, but that will require you to go through them as the middleman. This means the person performing the work doesn't actually work for you, and it will likely be more expensive than just finding a person who specializes in what you need at the moment. If the only work needed on the house is an upgraded electrical panel, go straight to a licensed electrician the same way you would go straight to a licensed plumber if you had a leak in your home. Overcomplicating simple tasks will only cost you more time and money in the long run.

Inspector

A home inspector can literally be the differentiating factor in walking away from a bad deal or getting stuck with a money pit where you are condemned to a lifetime of repairs and renovations. An inspector should not be confused with a contractor, even though both professionals may have similar knowledge. A home inspector walks through the house from top to bottom, or bottom to top, in search of anything and everything that might be wrong with the property. They are highly trained, and the really good ones will notice things even experienced contractors might miss.

An important note about inspections though is that the process is "non-invasive," meaning the inspector cannot damage the property in any way —'no pulling up the carpet to inspect the flooring beneath, no poking holes in the ceiling to look for water damage, or anything else that cannot be seen with the naked eye. They can remove the cover from an electrical panel so long as it can be replaced, inspect attics, or burrow into crawl spaces. Some inspectors will walk on the roof, while others might launch a drone or just inspect from the inside. If there is a certain service you are looking for, make sure to interview a few inspectors first and see who will do the specific things you have in mind.

Also, a home inspector is generally not liable if you still find something wrong after buying the house. They are not psychics and are unable to predict if and when something will break. Their reports will note the visible condition and age of mechanical systems, but some of these major components fail after ten years while others could last forty or more. Unless you can prove gross negligence on the inspector's part, accept whatever comes as part of the joy of owning real estate. Review their report thoroughly and ask as many questions as needed to feel comfortable in the likelihood of something going wrong in the near future and the magnitude of all major items they note.

Suppliers

The next component of your dream team might not necessarily be one specific person but rather the entire category of suppliers. Many might have just read that line and thought, *I've got Home Depot, Lowe's, and Ace – why the heck do I need to worry about suppliers?*

That is a great question. Many times, the larger, national brands are a perfect solution for what you need. They are low cost, high selection, and conveniently located, but they are also too big for their own good in many ways and cannot exercise the flexibility you need in a pinch. The rules and processes are written in stone, and your project's progress can get tied up in bureaucratic nonsense. One never knows when they are going to need a specialty part, service, or request that a national chain will not be able to fill, or at least not quickly. Some suppliers you should consider having a relationship with are:

- Hardware stores
- Plumbing supply stores
- Building supply (masonry and concrete) stores
- Flooring stores
- Window suppliers
- Electrical and lighting showrooms

Yes, any item that can be bought from any of those establishments can also be purchased from a national brand store. The question is, do they have the same selection and knowledge? If you have ever tried to get assistance from an employee in any of the large chain stores, chances are, you were left underwhelmed at best and walked out without what you needed at worst. The prices may be a little higher in the specialty outlets, but time is also money. Think about how much time is wasted with each trip to a store where you cannot get the information or equipment you need. The folks who work at the plumbing store will be better equipped to answer all your plumbing questions and order your specialty parts much faster and more reliably than their larger competitors.

Lenders

Next up is your lender. Unless you have enough cash on hand to avoid financing, you will need several reputable and reliable lenders to help get you to the finish line. Throughout this book, the term lender will be used interchangeably for the various sources of funding you might seek to leverage. It is a common misconception that all lenders are the same, so to avoid falling into the pitfall of choosing the wrong type for your particular need, we will cover each briefly.

- Mortgage Banker: A loan officer who works directly for a bank or lending institution and nowhere else. The only products and rates they can offer are set by the company, giving them very little flexibility in negotiating. An example of this would be the mortgage person at your local bank.
- Mortgage Broker: A loan officer who is not captive to one particular lender and can shop your loan to as many lenders as they have relationships with. Brokers can be a bit more expensive on their commission but also stand to get you better terms through their shopping.
- Direct Lender: These are companies that lend their own money but are not necessarily required to have a mortgage license since they are lending to entities and not individuals. They tend to have the most robust selection of loan programs, but fees, rates, and other terms can vary widely since they are less regulated than those issuing traditional mortgage products.
- Private Equity (PE): An individual or group of investors who have pooled their money for a like-minded purpose. Most PE investors will not entertain smaller deals, and their barrier for entry is often in the tens of millions. Most new investors will not have a chance here, but as your empire grows, the PE folks become increasingly valuable.
- Hard Money: Generally, this is someone lending their own money. The rates and terms will be the least advantageous of all the other options, but their approval guidelines are much more flexible. Just make sure you are fully aware of what you are signing up for because this is a segment not known for their forgiveness.

The time to shop for any of the professionals mentioned above is not after you have identified a deal or put it under contract – it is before you ever start looking. One of the worst feelings in the world is putting in countless hours of work finding deals and negotiating terms only to find out you cannot complete the transaction. Just because you *know* someone who does mortgages or works at a bank does not mean you have a lender on your team, and even if it does, there is no guarantee you are getting the best possible deal.

Most of the residential mortgages written in this country are regulated by the federal government through one of their many agencies such as Fannie Mae, Ginnie Mae, Freddie Mac, etc. Because of that, any traditional mortgage you try to get will be subject to roughly the exact same underwriting requirements no matter which institution your lender works for. Commercial mortgages, which can be obtained from all the individuals mentioned earlier, have more flexibility in their underwriting guidelines, and private lenders tend to offer the largest variety of loan programs. So, how do you know which one is right?

Have lots of conversations! Meet with as many different lenders as you can from all categories. Even hard money lenders can play a useful role in your real estate journey despite their higher-than-average rates and fees. Depending on the project you have lined up, the lender who was your best choice for the last loan could easily become the worst choice for the new loan. Some lenders do flips better than rentals, some do commercial better than residential, and so on. Here are some of the key differences you should ask each prospective lender about early on so you have a better idea of who to contact first when there is a need:
- Required minimum down payment
- Maximum loan-to-value (LTV)
- Maximum after-renovation-value (ARV)
- Minimum acceptable credit score
- Points charged
- Average underwriting time

Do not underestimate how important any one of those criteria can be or how much of an impact several of them together can make on your chances of getting the deal closed and keeping your costs down.

Get Real!

Everything in life is a trade-off, and real estate is no different. If you only have 10% to put down on a deal, but the lender with the best interest rate requires a 20% down payment, you must either pay the higher rate or find extra cash. The lender with the best rate and terms may not lend on the type of property you are buying. To avoid running into issues when it matters most, create an Excel sheet (an example is included in the Resources section) to organize all this information in one place so you can be sure to reach out to the right person as quickly as possible.

Insurance

This is such an important aspect of protecting your individual real estate holdings as well as your business and generational wealth. Sadly, when it comes time for a closing, most investors call up their insurance company of choice in search of the cheapest policy and get it bound as quickly as possible so as not to delay closing. Granted, the banks do not care much about what your policy does or does not cover, so long as it meets their minimum coverage limits and has them named as an "additional insured." However, a policy meeting the lowest possible requirements will likely only wind up helping the bank in the event of a total loss.

One of the key areas any good insurance agent should explain is the difference between insuring based on the appraised value of the property or using the rebuild value. The bank defers to the appraised value since their risk exposure in the transaction is limited to the amount they lent you. In the event of a loss, they will get paid in full, and you may be stuck with a vacant lot because a house purchased for $250K that was built 75 years ago can probably not be rebuilt for the same $250K, given the cost of construction materials and labor. In fact, the rebuild value is generally substantially higher, which also translates into a higher monthly premium. When your insurance policy allows for the cost of rebuilding the home, the bank will keep its original mortgage on the new construction and the full payout can be used to build a new, more modern house.

Flood zones are an area of the insurance policy where a good agent can be worth their weight in gold. The Federal Emergency Management Agency (FEMA) keeps a database of all properties in America that are considered to be in flood zones. When obtaining a mortgage, the lender will require you to buy additional flood insurance, but not all areas prone to flooding are classified as flood zones. This means you could unwittingly leave the flood coverage off your policy or actively opt to save money by skipping it. That might not be the case if an experienced agent can show you statistics on the flood map, past claims in the area, and any other historical data supporting the need for flood insurance. There is also a huge difference in how insurance companies classify flood damage that occurred as a result of something internal (broken pipe, leaky faucet, etc.) versus how they treat external flooding (natural disasters). Don't wait until it is time to place a claim to find out not all floods are handled the same way.

Another area of insurance we recently began focusing more on is renter's insurance, which are policies that protect the tenants. By no means do we, as the landlord, pay for them, but all leases state the renter is required to purchase their own or waive our liability to damages if something happens. In rental property situations, the tenants' belongings are not covered by the landlord's policy. As we recently found out the hard way, nor is loss of habitation. So, when we had a unit flood, and the tenant had to be relocated to a hotel for a few nights, the cost came out of our pocket. Considering the cost of a renter's policy is usually only a few (literally) dollars per month, it pays to educate your tenants as well.

Beyond insurance on the underlying properties, umbrella policies are worth considering for anyone with a substantial portfolio or significant personal wealth. Hopefully, you will have structured your entities in such a way that overall liability is reduced, but an umbrella policy covers a range of other assets above and beyond the normal insurable limits to ensure any lawsuits can be handled without you needing to take money out of your own pocket. Even though I have been a licensed property & casualty insurance agent, I will leave the rest of the explanations to your insurance agent of choice.

The last way a good insurance agent can help your business thrive is with business continuity and legacy planning. If you are the only active member of your real estate endeavors, what happens if something happens to you? If you die unexpectedly, will your children or spouse be capable of stepping in and taking over the daily operations? Chances are unlikely, which would leave them in a position of needing to liquidate the assets. Since this will not happen quickly or easily, the likelihood of them incurring operating losses while pending sale and receiving less than the properties might be worth are both substantial. A key man policy and buy-sell agreement are life insurance policies (disability insurance can be used as well) taken out on either the main contributor or on all partners. Should someone become incapacitated or die, the insurance policies will pay out lump sums to the other partners or their family members in accordance with the accompanying legal document your attorney drafted.

Lawyers

The great lawyers I work with on a regular basis would be offended if I failed to mention them, but I am sure they would quickly realize the reason for any oversight would be attributed to the less-than-positive connotation associated with their profession. In real estate, I would argue those stigmas go further than in any other field of law. If you are not working in an "attorney state," where lawyers are mandatory, you could either glance over this section or spend a few minutes understanding the difference a good lawyer can make in a transaction. To do that, let me tell you about one of my sales.

This was a personal rental property I chose to represent myself on – a mistake I will never make again. At least I had the presence of mind to lean on my usual dream team of real estate professionals to assist, and my go-to lawyer was absolutely a part of that. On the day of closing, when the buyer conducted their final walk-through, the main house plumbing trap in the basement was found to be spurting water. The buyer wanted to walk away, I wanted to fix the issue, and the attorneys were torn. After sitting in a conference room for hours going back and forth, my attorney informed me the only way the buyer would close was if I would allow the attorney to keep $40K in escrow to cover the potential cost of excavating the pipe and repairing it, instead of paying it to me at closing as I was expecting. For the record, $40K was roughly my entire profit on the deal.

Thankfully, I didn't let my emotions get the best of me. Instead, I called a few plumbers I knew, sent them pictures, and was assured the most a repair of this nature would run was $5K. I told my attorney I wanted to agree to the $40K holdback, with the condition that the final cost be determined by the average of three estimates from licensed plumbers. I would choose one plumber, the buyer would choose one plumber, and we would agree upon a third plumber. My lawyer thought I had lost my mind and advised me not to make such a risky deal. I laid out the facts for her, my knowledge of the situation, and the text message estimates from the plumbers I already spoke with. She ultimately told me that if I were any other client, she would have recused herself from the transaction because of the potential liability, but because it was me, she would support the move.

To make a very long story slightly shorter than it was, the plumbing work was completed three days after closing at a total cost of $1.5K. The buyer was thrilled, I was vindicated, and my lawyer was impressed. The reason I tell this story is to bring awareness to just how much control your lawyer can leverage during the course of a transaction. Most think they are smarter than the rest of the world and will not listen to reason or do anything outside of what law school told them was acceptable. Many more are lazy and do not feel they get paid enough for real estate transactions to absorb any potential risk. So, having a lawyer on your team who is willing to listen to you, advise on the dangers of whatever half-cocked scheme you may have in mind, and support you in writing is the key to debunking the real estate expression of "lawyers kill deals."

Title Agents

Title companies, or title insurance, as they are more commonly referred to, are responsible for making sure you are purchasing exactly what you think you are purchasing. The job of title agents working at these companies is to verify all legal representations made about the house and ensure nothing can come back to bite you in the behind later, which is where the insurance component of their name comes into play. At closing, they are providing insurance coverage to protect against errors or omissions on their part. Here is a quick list of some key items they address in their title report, which is then provided to the buyer, their attorney, and lender:

- Property boundaries: Letting you know if your property infringes on that of a neighbor, or vice versa.
- Lien searches: Making sure no one, such as a lender not already known about, a mechanic, or a taxing municipality, has not made a claim against the prior owner that would transfer over to you.
- Certificates of Occupancy: Verifying with the local municipality that there are no open permits or building code violations against the property, and that the legal description (property type, size, use, etc.) matches what the seller has represented in the sales contract.

In attorney states, the buyer's attorney will select the title insurance company. These selections are based on established business relationships, which usually means they have worked with the company before and can vouch for their work, they have received referrals from the title agent before, or a combination of both. None of this is to say you cannot specifically ask your attorney to use a specific title company of your choosing, and since you are paying the attorney for their services, there should be no pushback. If you live and invest in a state where attorneys are required, it is not quite as important to have your own title companies on standby. However, in non-attorney states, the title company is going to handle most of the closing process, so it is highly advisable to have a trusted local resource.

Appraiser

In almost all instances where a real estate appraiser is involved in a transaction, it will be at the behest of the bank or lender financing the project. Once upon a time, the lender could call their appraiser of choice for any given deal. Thanks to the financial crisis of 2008, that practice was eliminated, and now lenders must order all appraisals from an Appraisal Management Company (AMC). Each AMC will have several appraisers they work with, and when an appraisal order comes in, they choose amongst their providers as to who will get the job. Proximity to the property, area of expertise, and lead time to get the report done all factor into the decision, whereas monetary gain or affiliation with the lender or buyer do not, which was a solid step to reduce the number of fraudulent appraisals we once had.

Although you will likely have very few chances to use an appraiser in your network for any formal evaluation that can be presented to the bank, it still makes sense to have at least one or two good ones on your team. As someone whose entire profession is determining the value of real estate, an appraiser can be a key partner in helping you to arrive at how much to offer for a property or how much to sell one for. They have access to the same sales data that a real estate agent does, but they just happen to be much more skilled at evaluating it. That is by no means a knock on realtors, just a reality check. As mentioned earlier, it takes less than 100 hours to get a real estate license, but appraisers undergo thousands of hours of training and apprenticeship before receiving their license. They also do not make a whole lot of money for the service they provide, so anytime they can do side work without having to complete an entire report is a win-win for them and you.

Centers of Influence (COIs)

A COI is considered to be anyone with direct access to your ideal prospects. Some examples could be the local mailman who gets notified when mail is forwarded or addresses changed, painters and other professional home service providers who may be called in to upgrade the home prior to a sale, or even moving companies. Having a strong network of COIs will greatly help you find deals in real estate, and it does not cost you anything until a deal or lead is generated. The more COIs you have in your network who know what you are doing and what you are looking for, the more sets of eyes you have looking for potential deals. Some investors will pay these COIs upfront, but most promise a flat rate referral fee for every name they pass along or even a percentage of the commission for a closed transaction. Remember, 100% of 0 is 0, which means if they are making money, you are making money – money you never would have had without their referral – so share the love.

Accountant

The last, and arguably the most important, member of your dream team is a Certified Public Accountant (CPA). If you are on your first or second deal, you might be able to skate by with a bookkeeper or tax preparer, but as your business gets more sophisticated, you need to upgrade. Many people, myself included once upon a time, don't see a real distinction between a CPA and a tax preparer because, well, they can both prepare taxes. But when it comes to diving deep into all the potential tax liabilities, deductions, and reporting requirements that come with advanced real estate investing, a CPA is the only way to go. Think about it like going to your primary care physician after having a heart attack instead of a cardiologist. Yes, it's that serious.

More money can be made or lost on April 15th than almost any other day in the real estate world. Real estate affords a great many deductions and ways to minimize tax bills, but only when done properly. Every time you sell a house, it is subject to capital gains, either short-term or long-term. The income you make from your rental properties is all taxable as ordinary income to your company. To put that in perspective, let's assume you bought a property for $100K and sold it for $200K. Your effective capital gains are $100K, and the IRS will want roughly 20%-40% of that at the end of the year. Your CPA earns their living by helping you realize all the money you spent renovating that house (supplies, labor, carrying costs, etc.) as well as the overhead you had running your business. So, if you spent $75K (or can find a way to show you did), the effective gain is now only $25K. If you are in a 25% tax bracket, that changes your tax bill from $25K to $6,250!

No matter what road you are taking in the real estate world, do not walk it alone. Surround yourself with the best and brightest in their chosen fields and leverage their knowledge often. The best time to ask questions and get advice is before you spend any money or sign any contracts, not after. There is no prize for doing everything yourself other than burnout, frustration, and ultimately failure.

"Believing that nothing can do more toward the development of the highest attributes of good citizenship than the ownership by every family of its home, I am always glad to endorse effective efforts to encourage home ownership. Nothing better could happen to the United States than a very notable increase in the ownership of homes."

— Warren G. Harding

Chapter 2: Financing Strategies

It takes money to make money, or so the expression goes. There is no denying that having money definitely makes things in life easier, but it is not the only game in town. When dealing with real estate investments, the only limitation on how to complete a deal is the one living in your own mind. That's not to say you should blindly believe the chatter about never needing your own money to buy property or how many properties you can acquire in such a short period of time by strictly using other people's money. It's like the other old expression about not putting all your eggs in one basket. To go far in real estate, it is best to have a combination of viable financing strategies ranging from using none of your own money up to the bank's requirement of a 25% purchase price. To help you accomplish that, we will look at all the different ways we have personally secured real estate deals, as well as strategies our clients have used.

It is never too early for shopping lenders. Many brokers and lenders will claim to be able to handle any deal you bring them, only to find out in the moment of truth that they meant every deal *except* the one you have under contract for one reason or another. This is also why it is good to have a healthy mix of lenders including everything from the traditional national lenders a seller will feel all warm and fuzzy about up to the private lenders and hyper-regional banks. Keeping a database or spreadsheet with the names of each institution, who the lending contact is, and what programs they specialize in (not every product they offer) will save you time and stress when the time comes to make an offer. It is no different than when you were shopping for the best bank for your checking account needs, just do not fall victim to the trap of thinking your primary transactional bank will make the best lending bank – the two very rarely go hand in hand.

Mortgages

Let's start with the basics. Mortgages may be the most stringent and limiting, but they are also the most time-tested and widely accepted by potential sellers. Commercial mortgages are one of the easiest financing arrangements you can secure from a bank. They typically require at least 20-25% as a down payment but are not subject to any standardized underwriting guidelines, so there is more room for a bank officer to make a judgment call on your particular project even if it does not neatly fit into the box other more conventional lenders would require. These types of loans also allow for your LLC or corporation to own the property directly, whereas traditional residential mortgages do not. The downsides to these types of loans on top of the larger down payment requirement are that they usually come at higher interest rates than other types of loans and the repayment terms are generally 20 years instead of 30 years, making the monthly payments higher.

Another bank loan option would be the conventional residential mortgage that can be used for any single to four-family home. With down payment requirements starting as low as 5%, with some lenders and capping out at 20%, there is more leverage available than with commercial options. Other benefits of these loans are that they tend to come at lower interest rates and offer 30-year amortization, the period over which principal and interest payments are made, for a lower monthly payment. Because they are subject to federal underwriting criteria, you will not get the same level of flexibility with some other options, and a good deal might pass you by because of an underwriting technicality. Since these loans are meant for individuals, you will be hard-pressed to find a bank that allows you to purchase property in a company name.

Next on the list of bank options is one of the highest leverage choices but, unfortunately, also one of the most restrictive. Federal Home Administration (FHA) loans were created in 1934 as a way to promote more home ownership in America. With down payment options as low as 3.5%, there are not many other traditional options offering better leverage when you are low on cash. However, that's where the benefits end. FHA underwriting and appraisals are far more stringent than any other option, so much so that they will almost never be a viable option for any property that needs substantial renovation. FHA loans also come with private mortgage insurance (PMI) requirements that will substantially increase your monthly payment. Not only will you have no chance of buying the property in anything other than your personal name, but you will also be subject to residency requirements, meaning there is an expectation that you will live in the home for at least one year. This is not such a big deal if you intend to live there or if it is a multi-family home that you could try to pass off as a second residence, but that's a dangerous game to play and one that comes with mortgage fraud implications if you get caught.

If you or any co-borrower is an active or retired member of the US Armed Forces, you can take advantage of VA loans. Issued through the Department of Veteran Affairs, these loans were created to help our military members achieve home ownership through low down payments and other closing cost assistance. For something created with the best of intentions for a group absolutely deserving of it, it is a shame it ranks dead last on the list. VA loans are notoriously difficult to close due to the stringent paperwork and underwriting guidelines. Their appraisers make FHA inspections look like a walk in the park, and it can drag on for months before closing.

If you are fortunate enough to already own a home, there is also the strategy of using something called a home equity line of credit (HELOC), which is exactly what the name implies. If you have enough equity in your home (every bank's guidelines are different and changing all the time), a bank will give you a revolving line of credit to use for anything you see fit. Terms and structures also vary widely, but on average, you can expect to get a ten-year draw period where you can borrow and repay up to your credit limit as much as you want. Payments in the draw period are interest only, giving you the lowest possible repayment amount of any funds you advance for a down payment on a new property. If there is still an outstanding balance on the line after the draw period, it will be amortized into principal and interest payments over the next 20 years. On top of that, interest paid on the first $100,000 borrowed is tax deductible, thus lowering the cost of capital even further.

To fully understand the power of a HELOC, let's first define equity, which is the difference between what you owe on a property and what it is worth. If you owe $200K on your mortgage and the house appraises for $500K, then you have $300K in equity. Using an extremely conservative example, if the bank is willing to lend 50% loan-to-value (LTV), which is just industry jargon for saying the percentage of what the home is worth, in this case, you would be able to secure a HELOC for $50K. Here's the math:

$500,000 (Appraisal value) X 50% (LTV) = $250,000
$250,000 – $200,000 (Mortgage amount remaining) = $50,000

While this is not meant to be a handbook on mortgages, there are a few non-negotiable requirements you will need to meet in order to have any hope of securing traditional financing. Credit is one of the biggest issues in all of real estate, although with traditional mortgage products, credit scores in the high 500s and low 600s still have a chance of being acceptable so long as there are no derogatory records or collections on your credit report. The next item up for consideration will be your debt-to-income (DTI) ratio. Banks will only lend if you can prove your monthly expenses (everything related to the purchase of the home and other items on your credit report such as credit cards and car loans) are less than 45% of your gross monthly income. The value of the collateral will be the final checkpoint, with the subject property needing to appraise for at least what the purchase contract states, as the bank will not approve a mortgage for more than the house is worth. If it appraises for higher, that's okay – it's a sign you made a good deal. Having your finger on the pulse of these numbers in your own life will go a long way in deciding how much time to spend on traditional options.

Leverage

Another bank strategy that could prove useful if you have money invested in the stock market and don't want to pull it out for one reason or another is a margin account. We won't go into the reasons against it or for it but rather explore something known as a margin loan, or collateralizing the assets held in your investment accounts. Unlike the traditional use of margin accounts to "borrow" money from your broker to buy more stock than you could otherwise afford at a set interest rate, collateralizing your assets allows the broker to loan you a percentage of your investment portfolio to use how you see fit without having to liquidate any holdings. Depending on the type of security you own, the broker in question, and current market conditions, these loans can often cost less than real estate-secured loans, but they also come at the expense of tying up your investment dollars until the loan is repaid.

The self-directed IRA is another one of real estate investing's best-kept secrets. Almost everyone has heard of Traditional and Roth IRAs, but a fraction of that have heard of the self-directed option – CPAs included. There are plenty of great books written on the topic, so we won't go into a technical lesson. Instead, we will focus on the benefits. While the other IRA options are limited to bank and investment products, a self-directed IRA provides you the ability to purchase anything (precious metals, collectibles, real estate, etc.) and hold your purchased assets to the same tax-deferred benefits as your other retirement accounts.

So, let's say you have $100K sitting in an IRA or old 401K not doing much. You put the funds into a self-directed IRA, which you then do not have to pay taxes on, and use it as a down payment on a $400K house that you sell in five years for $500K. The $100K profit you made goes back into your self-directed IRA and is not subject to any taxable gains unless you make an unqualified distribution from it. Now, you have $200K available (with the original $100K, plus the $100K profit) and could repeat the same process – twice! The same holds true if

41

you use the funds for rental properties, as all of the rental income would be considered IRA gains and thus not presently taxable.

Business Lending

Business lending is another area to focus on as you get more established, which is also why it makes sense to get your legal entity established early on in your real estate career. While commercial mortgages are going to likely require a minimum of two years of business tax returns, there are some other options available to businesses through banks with shorter history requirements. The first is the business line of credit (BLOC), which is similar to a home equity line of credit except it is either unsecured or secured by other assets your business might own outside of real estate. Accounts receivable, equipment, inventory, and even company-owned vehicles can all be considered collateral for a BLOC, and depending on the bank, you might be able to secure a modest line of credit after being in business for as little as six months. The terms and conditions may not be as advantageous as a HELOC, but you are also not being asked to put your home on the line.

Another business option is called a bank statement loan or cash flow loan, and it is exactly what it sounds like. Business lenders, private companies, and not your traditional brick-and-mortar banks will lend you a lump sum of money or a revolving line of credit based on the activity in your business bank statements. The key information they are looking for is the amount of deposits flowing through the checking account each month and what the average monthly balance is for any given three months. Generally, credit requirements are very low, and personal guarantees are not required, both of which are huge advantages. However, if you sit down and calculate the cost of capital, these APRs often run between 30%-50% and will require substantial weekly or monthly repayments. This will scare off most people who have been trained to only look at APR in a bubble and run away if the rate seems too high, but the other side of the equation should include how much profit can be made by taking the loan in the first place.

By no means is this an endorsement of blindly taking a loan with such high rates and fees, but for the savvy investor, it can be the difference between closing on an amazing deal or letting someone else capture it.

As an example, let's say you found a property you intend to buy, renovate, and resell, also known as a flip. As the buyer, you purchase the house for $200K. To make the down payment of 25%, you borrow the money from a lender who offers a 50% interest rate.

$200,000 (Purchase price) X 25% = $50,000 (Down payment amount)

$50,000 (Down payment) X 50% interest = $25,000

$50,000 (Original down payment) + $25,000 (Interest) = $75,000 (Amount to pay back to the lender)

After putting a down payment of $50K on the $200K house, you still owe $150K, which is the balance on the mortgage. In addition, the renovations to flip the house cost you $50K, but those renovations allow you to resell the house for $300K. Let's look at the amount of equity you have after the sale.

$300,000 (Resale price) − $150,000 (Mortgage balance) = $150,000 (Gross profit)

$150,000 (Gross profit) − $50,000 (Renovations) − $75,000 (Amount to pay back to the lender) = $25,000

You are still ahead by $25,000 in gained equity, not to mention the profit you will make every month on the rent roll, which is the total amount of rent your tenants pay in any given month. Is it risky? Of course. But sometimes you need to take calculated risks to make money, and in this scenario, you accomplish this without using a penny of your own money.

Creative

Now that we've covered just about every traditional option I know of (or at least can remember), it is time to get creative. We are going to do it in order of most risky – but also most accessible – up to the safest but hardest to achieve. The first option falls into a similar category of the business bank statement loans, and that is the credit card cash advance. Yes, you read that right. Even though most credit card companies will charge a flat fee of 3%-5% on any advance amount plus an APR of 30% and up on average, the same rules of deal evaluation apply, which we will discuss in more detail in Chapter 7. In a pinch, you might have credit cards with decent limits, so if a deal comes along unexpectedly, and you are unable to secure any other financing options quickly enough, this can easily bridge the gap.

The next creative financing strategy that is slightly less risky than cash advances would be the use of "hard money," a term for unconventional real estate financing that has a misunderstood stigma surrounding it. Hard money gets lumped in with borrowing money from loan sharks or other dangerous individuals, and while some may fall into that category, the large majority are less interested in breaking your kneecaps than they are making higher-than-normal returns on their money and potentially taking ownership of your investment property should you default on the loan. At the time of writing this, there are dozens, if not hundreds, of hard money brokers who specialize in matching lenders with investors as well as lending institutions that will work directly with investors.

While hard money programs have traditionally been focused more on flip investors, many new programs have been rolled out to cater to the rental market as well. Since there are too many options to list, with new ones getting added every day, it would be impossible to review the pros and cons for each. What we will focus on is the major dangers of these loans. Much like other options, the fees and interest rates on hard money loans are going to be higher than more traditional options. What can make these even more predatory though is the term of the loan. Many of these lenders will help fund up to 100% of the purchase price with some money toward renovations but will require the loan to be paid back in as little as 90 days, but on average six months to one year. If you are unable to either sell the property or refinance the loan with a more traditional lender, they will be within their rights to take possession of the property and sell it themselves. Unlike major banks where the foreclosure process can take months, these companies act swiftly, and any delay on the project can mean watching everything you worked for get ripped away.

The safest and my favorite creative financing option is seller financing, commonly referred to as "holding paper" or a "purchase money mortgage," in which the seller acts as either the sole bank in the transaction or a secondary lender, depending on whether they lend you the full amount or a percentage of it. The first question we ask on every one of our deals is whether or not the seller is willing to hold paper, which allows us to search for properties that might otherwise be over our budget. Having only $50K cash on hand would normally mean the highest purchase we could consider is somewhere between $200K-$300K. If a seller is willing to hold paper in some capacity, it could raise our maximum purchase price anywhere in the range of hundreds of thousands of dollars.

There are two ways this can work out. Let's start with a best-case scenario, where the owner will hold 100% of the financing. For full transparency, this does not happen often, which we will get into, but it never hurts to ask. In a 100% scenario, the owner is basically turning over all ownership responsibilities to you, while also granting all rights to collect rent or any other profits as well. If you currently own property, and even if you don't but you know a bit about real estate, you might be wondering why anyone in their right mind would agree to this. This is a valid thought, which is why most don't, but you never know what someone is going through. There are hundreds of reasons someone might not want to or might not be able to continue managing their own property that could lead them to this point. Whether it be moving, lack of funds to maintain the property, or sheer disgust with owning the property – their situation becomes your advantage. Granting 100% financing also makes them the sole lien holder on the property, and in the event you default on monthly payments, they can foreclose on the property and take it back the same way a bank would.

The next option is to arrange a scenario where the current owner operates in the same capacity as a bank. As the buyer, you commit to making a down payment at closing, which can vary widely depending on preference and need, while the seller holds the remainder of the sales price in the form of a private mortgage. The mechanics are the same as in the 100% financing strategy, but it also gives the seller more options and peace of mind. It is not always possible for them to commit to 100% financing due to outstanding mortgages, liens, relationships with other owners, and even their own comfort level, so showing them you are willing to put up some of your own money can separate your offer from other investors looking to take greater advantage of the situation with hardball negotiation tactics over price.

The last and most common option, at least in my experience, is where the seller agrees to hold an amount the bank considers to be sufficient for a down payment, then they finance the difference. So, in the event of a commercial mortgage, the seller would hold 25%, while the bank finances the other 75%. There is one caveat to this option though, which is making sure your lender will accept the seller financing as part of the down payment. Most national lenders will not entertain any seller financing situations, and even some of the smaller more flexible lenders will want to see you put some "skin in the game" before they will lend. Depending on market conditions and circumstances, you might even find a lender who will do this in one instance but not another. All the more reason to have a number of trusted lending partners on standby, so you can shop each deal to secure the best possible terms and not risk having a great no-money-down deal pass you by.

There is also a strategy called the seller's concession, which is where the seller agrees to a higher purchase price under the agreement that the extra money will be credited toward the buyer's closing costs. This is a great way to reduce how much cash you need to close the deal, with very little downside to the seller since the money is not coming out of their pocket. There are limits to much you can ask for, generally 3%-6% of the total purchase price, and the house must appraise at the higher amount, including the concession, or else the bank will not allow it. On a home purchase of $500K, asking for a seller's concession can save you anywhere between $15K-$30K – cash you are now free to use on another deal!

An example of just how powerful seller financing can be for all parties involved would be our recent acquisition of a 6+ acre parcel of land with three single-family residences on it. All the buildings needed varying degrees of renovation, and because there were multiple structures involved, the deal could have been evaluated as a flip or a cash flow investment. The sellers were looking to get $450K, which never would have shown up on our radar since we never paid that much money for what was technically a three-family property. However, we had worked with a realtor in the listing office before, and she not only saw the potential for us to renovate and then hold in our portfolio, but she also knew the seller was highly motivated to sell. The ARV of this particular property was $575K, which would have left a slim profit margin at a purchase price of $450K. After negotiating them down to $400K and convincing them to hold 25% of that while one of our three banks lent us the other 75%, we now have found equity and all three units rented at fair market rent for an additional monthly income.

Take a second to consider the example above. Everyone wants to get a good deal, and we are very much the same. However, it is impossible to place a value on the benefits seller financing brings. The more flexible a seller is willing to be on the terms, the more you stand to gain. When we know the seller is willing to entertain holding paper, I will create what I like to call an offer ladder. That ladder basically consists of the prices I would be willing to pay based on what the seller will concede to beyond just price. For this particular deal, my offer ladder looked something like this:

- Option 1: Seller holds 100% of the mortgage at a purchase price of $450,000.
- Option 2: Seller holds 25% of the mortgage at a purchase price of $400,000.
- Option 3: Seller holds no paper, and we use a traditional bank at a purchase price of $350,000.

By taking this approach, we are allowing the seller to feel like they are in more control of the outcome. They can easily say none of those options work for them and wait for someone to come along with a better offer, and that is okay! If they find another buyer, we move onto the next deal. If a few weeks have gone by without an acceptable offer, they can come back to us or us to them – with a potentially lower offer. When there are options on the table, the seller can weigh the pros and cons of each offer and feel a degree of comfort in knowing they did not just take the first offer out of desperation. I would also point out we had no intention of going with Option 3, even if they were okay taking such a low number. It was more for illustrative purposes, but they did not need to know that!

Private Equity

Private equity (PE) can take many forms and often falls under a combination of all the other lending types we spoke about, but as a rule of thumb, they are only looking for the multi-million dollar deals – meaning don't go there for help buying a $100K single-family home. You may or may not be familiar with the term from its many uses in modern culture and investment lingo, but in reality, it is not that difficult to understand – the challenge is in qualifying for it. Private equity can come in the form of an individual investor or a group of investors who have pooled their capital together for like-minded investments. It is kind of like seller financing, only the PE investors are shouldering most of the risk instead of the seller.

There are countless platforms out there offering PE options to real estate investors, but for the sake of simplicity, we will look at an example almost everyone has probably heard of – *Shark Tank*. Every *shark* is a private equity investor looking for the deals they believe to be the most profitable while aligning with their overall investment strategy. The terms they offer each contestant are quite unique and all based on what they expect their overall return to be. This is the same for PE investors in real estate. Just because one particular group of investors disliked your proposal does not mean you cannot find another that is more aligned with your strategy. Some investors prefer a certain asset class, others a geographic area, and the list goes on. Grow a thick skin and learn that the word "no" is a good thing to hear – at least someone is listening to you!

Infinite Banking

Out of the gate, let me be clear – this strategy requires some money and a willingness to invest in whole life insurance. There was a time when I would have thought this to be heretic, but today, I realize all vehicles exist for a reason. The benefits of traditional whole life insurance are as widely disputed in professional circles as they are in consumer circles. Many other things are equally contested, which brings me to my point. Look at your individual situation before deciding on the right strategy. For the sake of being thought-provoking, we will spend a quick second diving into how this works, but for a more comprehensive explanation of how this works and if it is a good fit for you, contact one of those insurance agents we spoke about in the last chapter.

Whole life insurance has a very bad reputation, and I cannot personally or professionally argue it is a bad thing. It is incredibly profitable for the insurance company, the agent, and anyone else involved. BUT, if used wisely, it does not need to have any correlation to your own mortality. These kinds of insurance policies allow for tax-deferred growth most have never imagined possible. Why? Because most do not have enough money to make this strategy viable – nor is it being recommended on a large scale.

If you do choose to do a buy-sell agreement or a key man policy as spoken about in the last chapter, this could benefit you. When any assets, especially real estate derived in this example, are invested in a life insurance policy, you benefit from the same protections an average purchaser does: the premiums could be tax deductible, the amount you borrow from the policy is tax-free, and there are no limits to how often you can borrow from the policy so long as the funds are available. After speaking with an insurance specialist, double-check with your CPA about the potential tax benefits and how they would apply in your specific situation.

"Art, like real estate, is half science, half gut. We go to a lot of art fairs. I have two full-time art experts who help me make all the decisions about how to build the corporate and personal collection and what we put in our developments. We don't let interior designers pick art for us."

— Jorge M. Pérez

Chapter 3: Deal Finding

Deal finding is arguably the hardest part of real estate in general. There will always be competitors trying to list a home for sale if they are licensed agents, buy it themselves if they are investors, or get it under contract first if they are wholesalers. Every market and every homeowner is different, so despite what the so-called "experts" say, there is no magic formula for finding deals. To be successful in real estate, you must be disciplined, focused, and resilient. This is not a business where you can put in a few hours a week and make any significant money. Working less than twenty hours a week will likely not yield you any return for several weeks or months at a time.

Ultimately, the method of deal finding that works best will depend on a given investor's preferred investment strategy, the market they operate in, and the resources at their disposal. I like to classify resources into three main categories: time, assets, and network. It is impossible to be successful in real estate without dedicating at least one of the three to uncovering deals, but optimally, you should be able to find a balance between two of the categories. When I was working a full-time job, I had access to capital and a network of people who I came in contact with daily, but I had no free time. As a new real estate investor, you may find yourself with only time on your side, in which case you should first focus on growing your network or generating some other source of assets to help fund your business. The best thing about real estate is you get to decide which mix works best for you and your family or situation.

Observation

The good news is, money – and by money, I mean cold, hard cash – was not one of the things we just listed as a requirement for real estate. It is definitely helpful to have a budget to get your business off the ground, but good old-fashioned elbow grease can substitute for dollars in the early stages. One of the best techniques for building a database of potential sellers is known as "driving for dollars," and outside of money for gas, it does not cost anything. The premise of this strategy is to drive around the neighborhoods where you are hoping to acquire deals and identify properties that might be in distress. This could look like:

- Overgrown lawn
- Broken windows
- Cracked pavement
- Deteriorating roof
- Peeling or faded exterior paint

The list goes on and on. These conditions are attractive to a real estate investor because they usually signify the owner is not fully invested in the property or they are experiencing one of three challenges. The first and most obvious is money problems, and this is found most commonly with elderly or disabled owners who live on fixed budgets. Homeownership can be expensive and too much of a burden to keep up with over time. These owners will sometimes know they need to sell but have not taken the steps to do so because they do not think anyone will want to pay a fair price for the home.

The second reason could be the fear of finding a new place to live when that home is all they have ever known. The key is to understand what their true situation is. Potential sellers are people first and foremost. They have feelings, beliefs, and motivations beyond just getting out of a bad situation or making a quick dollar. Taking the time to understand what is important to someone who falls into one of these three categories will not only separate you from every other shark trying to separate them from their home, but it will help guide your next steps. The hurdle for a seller could be as simple as not having the money to pay to keep their belongings in storage or as severe as having liens and judgments against them that will ultimately eat into or erase any profit they may have made. You might be able to help some people, but there will always be situations where all you can do is move on.

The third reason for disrepair could also just be because it is an absentee owner situation, where the occupants are merely tenants and have not bothered notifying the owner about the repairs needed. This happens all the time in rental situations and quickly becomes a huge problem for a landlord. While no landlord wants to be bothered with every minor maintenance issue a tenant brings up, especially since some requests are just outrageous, items pertaining to the structural integrity of the property or posing quality-of-life issues are extremely important. Tenants may think asking the landlord to make these repairs will result in increased rent to offset the charges, or they may prefer not to have the landlord come on-site to find out they are hoarders or running a meth lab (no, that is unfortunately not a joke). When you bring these issues to the owner's attention, you are allowing them to decide whether they want to address them or if it would be easier to sell – to you!

Based on the scenarios we covered above, the reason for disrepair could also be a result of the owner being unwilling to address the maintenance items. This generally happens when there is a contentious situation with a tenant or an internal dispute with other owners on how to best proceed with allocating funds for repair. No matter what the reason is for the refusal to fix the items, it provides the opportunity to step in and buy the house so they are absolved of the headache. Several roadblocks might still exist with business partners who refuse to sell or by acquiring a property with problem tenants, which we will discuss in a later chapter, but if selling has crossed their mind, you have the chance to appear as their savior instead of a greedy investor looking to profit from their misfortune.

Marketing

Postcards and other mailers are other low-cost ways of getting in front of large numbers rather quickly. Whether you custom print your own material, fill it out by hand, and drop it in the mailbox or have a fulfillment company do everything from start to finish, this strategy will generally run you less than sixty cents per postcard or $60 for every hundred cards mailed. Without using any specialized or costly software to generate lists, you can easily pull up a map of your target neighborhoods on Google and manually start creating databases with addresses. You can then mail generic cards to "homeowner" or take the extra step of using a website like www.truepeoplesearch.com to research the owner's name – for free. If you have a little money and time is in short supply, there are plenty of companies that sell lists of names and addresses for pennies on the dollar as well.

The next free method for deal hunting ties in closely with the mailing strategy we just spoke with, and that is phone calls, texts, and emails. You can skip the mailers and go straight to calling the people you added to your database, but it will also prolong the sales cycle. People are being solicited for anything and everything more than ever before, which makes your cold text, call, or email indistinguishable from all the other targeted marketing efforts they receive. Recent studies have shown the average consumer needs to be "touched" almost 26 times before they will engage with a person or company. Mailing a postcard before reaching out becomes the first touch in that sequence and provides a conversation starter that could sound something like, "Hey, Mr. Smith. This is Matt from Time Away Group, and I just wanted to follow up on the postcard we mailed out last week."

Chances are and experience has proven, they never looked at the postcard or do not even remember seeing it lumped in with all the other junk mail they received, but it makes you appear more familiar and piques their curiosity as to what the postcard contained. So, your second touch becomes the follow-up on the postcard. I personally like varying my contact methods and spacing them out to stay top of mind without being a nuisance.

Here is what a standard follow-up sequence for me generally looks like when using postcards:
- Touch 1: Mail the postcard.
- Touch 2: Follow up with a text 7 days later.
- Touch 3: Send a second text 7 days after the first.

- Touch 4: Send a third text 7 days after the second text.
- Touch 5: Make a phone call 3 days after the third text.

After the fifth touch, I will tailor my remaining follow-up based on whether or not I was able to have a conversation with them or if it was just a voicemail. Any type of interaction, whether it be on the phone or in text is invaluable – that is the gold you are trying to mine. Even if they say they are not interested, that is okay! Remember, this is a long game, and you still have plenty more touches to go. Asking simple questions, like "Would it be okay if we stayed in touch to see if anything changes in a few months?" or "Can you think of anyone else in your area who may be thinking of selling?" can grant you the permission to follow up with them again or possibly get a qualified lead.

I always like to subscribe to the philosophy that there is no such thing as a "no," only "not now," unless of course they specifically say not to contact them anymore or to be removed from your list. Then, it is best to honor the request and avoid getting in legal trouble. Otherwise, all of these conversations have just become future prospects. The real key to making this work though is to keep meticulous records with notes and follow-up dates. When someone gives you permission to call again in three weeks and you never do, money is getting left on the table. After speaking and exchanging texts several times over the course of months and years, the prospect no longer views you as a cold solicitation but rather a warm resource they have never met.

The fortune is in the follow-up. I have personally witnessed brokers and investors stay in touch with prospects for ten years or more through regular outreach and finally land a deal after all that work. Ideally, the sales cycle won't usually be quite that long, but if you are in this for the long haul, the consistency you put into this process will build a healthy pipeline and pay dividends for years to come. You can use anything from a fancy CRM (Customer Resource Management) system to a basic spreadsheet to manage your follow-ups. There is no right or wrong answer, just make sure you are putting in the effort and actively reaching out according to the notes from the last conversation, or you run the risk of them doing business with someone else. People have short-term memories, so it is your job to make yourself the first and only person on their minds when it comes to selling their property.

Technology

Another free prospecting option many investors tend to overlook because of the perceived constraints with "on-market" deals is Zillow – and that is a huge mistake. At the time of writing this, Zillow is the most popular real estate platform in the United States. When a realtor lists a property on the MLS, it automatically feeds over to Zillow. When a homeowner decides to try selling their home without an agent, Zillow is usually the first place they turn. So, while it is true this option does not provide a competitive advantage over other buyers, the sophisticated tailoring of Zillow's search tools can still give you a leg up.

Time kills deals, and nothing could be more true in real estate. The sooner you can make contact with a potential seller, the greater your chances of getting the deal. Sellers are often surprised when they get a phone call within minutes of listing their property. It almost feels like you are a psychic or so good at what you do that they must speak to you. You don't need to be psychic to learn how to use Zillow's instant alert feature that allows you to select the criteria you are interested in and set up automation emails. I get anywhere from 10-30 real-time listing alerts every day from Zillow in all the areas I do business. More than a few deals have come from being the first person to reach a seller, making a great impression, and staying in constant contact with them until a contract is signed.

Beyond the free and low-cost strategies commonly used by people new to the business, there are also sophisticated software programs capable of providing volumes of data and contact information in seconds. Some of these programs are better than others, and they can vary wildly in price from one to the next. Certain platforms are only available to licensed real estate professionals and others are open to the general public. At the end of the day, each one provides roughly the same information, so it will be an individual decision to evaluate the pricing and features to see which best suits your needs.

Two of my favorite tools are the platforms Propstream and Remine. I currently use Remine because it comes free with my local MLS membership, but prior to that, I used Propstream with an equal level of success. These platforms allow you to sort search criteria in so many different ways that the information can quickly become overwhelming. After narrowing down to a geographic area, it will be important to understand what each of the filters does and why they are important to you.

Let's look at some of the most impactful criteria and why:
- Property Value: the estimated fair market value (FMV) of the homes in your search. This is used to ensure you are only finding properties within your desired price range. Anything over budget will be a waste of time, and anything too inexpensive might not have serious profit potential.
- Home Equity: the estimated amount of money an owner would get after selling the house. This is important because the more equity available, the more options the seller has for relocating. Less equity can indicate a new owner or someone in financial trouble.
- Ownership Time: a more straightforward metric than home equity but one that should be used in conjunction with that filter. If someone has owned a home for 20+ years but has no equity, you can more safely assume they are struggling financially.
- Absentee: a filter that lets you know the owner of the home does not live in the home. They are likely an investor, or it is a second home.
- Building type: the distinction as to whether a property is a single-family, multi-family, condo, or other property type.

- Mortgage Rate: a filter that can allow you to add value for a potential seller by showcasing how they could save money by selling to avoid paying a high rate or by referring them to your lending partners for a potential refinance. Granted that might not help you in the moment, but your partners will appreciate it, and the owner will become a trusted contact you can stay in touch with for future business.
- Distressed: everyone's favorite filter indicating whether the property is a pre-foreclosure, short sale, or foreclosure. These are the most profitable deals but also the hardest to obtain, so we will discuss these in the next section.

Having access to all this data can seem overwhelming, even insurmountable at times, but don't let that stop you. Start by picking one or two of the filters that would be the most helpful in narrowing down the best possible options. For example, use the property value filter to only show homes within your budget in combination with the property type filter, so you can hone in on single-family homes if you are flipping or multi-family homes if you are a cash flow investor. Data is only as good as what you do with it. You will need to determine why each of the filters discussed above are important in your strategy and employ them accordingly. You should also track the results of your calls so you can identify patterns of where the best outcomes seem to happen.

Also, keep in mind this data is all pulled from public records and is fairly accurate most of the time, but there will be times when it is wrong, and that's okay. It is better to find out at the qualification stage when all you have invested is a few dollars and the time it takes to make a phone call. Either cross that property off your list or make the most of the conversation with the homeowner to see if there might be any other opportunity available. Just because it was not what you were looking for does not preclude it from being profitable.

There are so many more ways you can go about finding deals – divorce records, foreclosure auctions, surrogate court filings for the recently deceased, and the list goes on and on – but we would need an entire book dedicated solely to the topic. You could choose to drill down and specify one particular source of leads, incorporate a few, or try to work them all at the same time. The only thing that matters and directly contributes to your success in the real estate business is how much time you put in every day to generate leads and work the follow-up system.

Distressed Deals

There is certainly money to be made when you can find one of these deals, but there are literally hundreds of investors fighting over the same ones. I still remember when I worked at a bank, and people would come in asking how they could access our list of bank-owned properties. They could not understand how we did not have access to these lists since they read a book on foreclosures or attended a seminar where it was made to seem like banks are just waiting to give these properties away. While it may seem counterintuitive for a bank to not make this part of the process easy, it is a fact of life. Banks are giant bureaucratic entities, but their foreclosure departments are also secretive and elusive.

Every distressed deal is different. Depending on the specific nature of the property in question, it could be easier or harder to secure one. The three classifications of distressed deals are pre-foreclosure, short sale, and foreclosure.

First is pre-foreclosure, or the stage where a homeowner has just defaulted on their mortgage, but the bank has not yet begun any proceedings to take back the property. This generally does not happen until at least two payments are missed. At this stage, the bank is still looking for ways to help get the owner current since they are only in the business of taking ownership in real estate when it's the last resort. These options could include a forbearance or loan modification, so it is important to realize they still have options at this point and might not welcome your attempts at profiting from their misfortune. When contacting these homeowners, or ones at any stage of foreclosure for that matter, be polite and respectful while seeing if there is an opportunity for all parties to benefit.

After a home has been in pre-foreclosure with no suitable outcomes for the bank or homeowner, it will move to the short sale stage, which is where the bank will entertain letting the homeowner sell the property for less than what is owed on it. These are incredibly difficult situations because everyone involved is losing something. The bank will not get the full amount on the outstanding mortgage, and the owner will walk away without a penny since the bank gets to keep everything. All these deals must be approved by the bank, not the owner, so your negotiating power as a buyer is severely reduced. The process is long, frustrating, and often ends with the deal falling apart, but for those who have the patience and intestinal fortitude to brave the process, there is money to be made here.

To stress just how long and frustrating this process can be, let's look at one of my poor clients. She was in her late seventies and had been fighting with her bank for almost ten years because she struggled to make payments. They offered a variety of modifications along the way, stuck her in pre-foreclosure a few times, and then one day decided they would entertain short sale offers. Had the home been in good condition, it would have appraised for around $700K, but in its current condition, we all knew that was a long shot. She owed the bank around $400K, so I advised her to list at $540K in the hopes of paying them off and getting her a few dollars to move to Florida. On the first day listed, we received an all-cash offer for $541K. Slam dunk, right?

Well, not really. The bank took forever to review the terms. They changed the short sale negotiator three times throughout the process, in each instance asking us to resubmit everything. As we were jumping through their hoops, interest and penalties continued accruing on the mortgage. After sitting in contract for over a year (yes, you read that right), the $541K was no longer enough to pay the bank and realtors, so we were asked to waive our commissions – which we begrudgingly did. The bureaucratic machine still could not get their act straight and ultimately sent the home to auction. The one sliver of hope in this story is that the buyers we had in contract managed to buy the house at that auction for the sweet price of $400K. In the process, our client was left homeless and penniless, the bank got less money than they would have had they made the short sale work, and both realtors worked on the deal for free over a fifteen-month span. The only winner here was the buyer, who ultimately got a $141K discount, even if it did come at the expense of much time and emotional distress.

Foreclosure, also known as "bank owned" or "real estate owned (REO)," is the final stage of the default process, where the owner has been removed and the bank or lender now owns the property. They generally hire property management companies to oversee the maintenance and upkeep of the home while it is pending sale and engage a realtor to sell it. In an effort to curb inside deals, which are where the property is given to a private investor at the lowest possible price, bank-owned properties will often go to auction. Sometimes these auctions are conducted by submitting your bid through the listing agent and waiting to hear back, and others are more transparent, being listed through online auction sites, such as Hubzu, where the current bid is shown until the end of the auction window when it gets awarded to the highest bidder. There are many advantages to foreclosed properties, but it's important to note they are not always in the best condition, and oftentimes, you will be expected to bid without ever having a chance to inspect the interior condition.

I want to stress that last sentence to the highest degree. I cannot think of any circumstance where I would purchase a property without seeing the interior, but simply getting access does not mean you are in the clear. Owners who are in the foreclosure process can be very bitter. It is already understandable for the place to be in disrepair due to their financial hardship, but there are those who will actively destroy the property. A relative of mine bought a foreclosure a few years ago after conducting a thorough inspection only to find out when they moved in that the prior owner had poured quick-dry cement down every drain in the house, effectively destroying the plumbing system and adding a significant cost to the renovations. This is just one horror story of what some people will do, so always be prepared for extra costs when buying distressed properties.

Another type of distressed deal is a tax lien situation, but this would be considered a long play because as long as the owner keeps paying back the lien amount, you cannot acquire the property. Unlike a mortgage that eventually can be paid off, property taxes never go away. In fact, over time, they will only continue rising. This means a homeowner can find themselves in a potential tax lien situation anytime during ownership that can result in the municipality placing a lien on the property. We won't go into great detail on this topic since there are plenty of great books written on the subject, but the process goes something like this:
- The homeowner misses a tax payment.
- The municipality places a lien on the home.
- The lien is sold to investors at auction (at damn good interest rates, depending on the state).
- The tax lien holder is granted ownership of the property if the owner defaults on making principal and interest payments.

Unlike other types of distressed deals, there is very little downside in a tax lien other than the waiting period. On the upside, you are acquiring ownership interest in real estate for generally a fraction of what it is worth. Imagine paying $25K to cover someone's delinquent taxes. You will earn anywhere between 8%-16% interest from the delinquent party until it is repaid. Now, imagine the house is worth $250K, and the owner stops making payments. You just paid 10% of what the house is worth (in this case, the $25K you used to buy the lien) and instantly gained $225K in equity. As part of a well-balanced real estate strategy, tax liens are a must for any investor with extra cash.

The million-dollar question with distressed deals is always the same – how the heck do I find them? Unfortunately, there is no easy answer to that question. Free sites like Zillow do offer some search options to filter these properties out, but by this time, every other investor has access to the same information. Be wary of paid sites and services promising access to lists of pre-foreclosures and foreclosures. More often than not, this information is outdated or inaccurate. If you already have access to a paid subscription such as Remine or Propstream, start by using their filters to gauge accuracy. If you have extra money to burn and the time to comb through hundreds of inaccurate leads in search of the golden ticket, then go ahead and sign up for a few services to see for yourself. Otherwise, get familiar with the local courts and their online portals. Why? All legal actions taken by banks or for tax lien purposes are recorded in local court documents and made available to the public for free or at a nominal cost.

Pre-foreclosures and foreclosures are filed as "lis pendens," which is Latin for "pending legal action." Depending on how often these records are filed and made available to the public, you will have access to this information long before data-mining companies scrape and repackage it at a cost to you. Some court systems may charge a nominal fee to access the records by day or month, but many are also free. There might not always be a way to search for exactly what you want though, so you may have to review every court filing in search of the foreclosures. I tend to look at this as a benefit and not a deterrent though because you never know what other filings could prove useful. The local courts are also where bankruptcies, mechanics liens, and divorce decrees are filed as well – all of which could provide access to other types of distressed deals and motivated sellers.

Once you know where to get the leads, the fun (or hard part, depending on how you look at it) begins – reaching out to these folks. As mentioned earlier, these are very delicate situations, and above all else, you need to proceed with empathy and compassion for the situation these homeowners are in. Chances are, they already know they are in trouble, are likely working with an attorney, and possibly already have a plan to get out of the situation. So, don't be surprised if you are not instantly viewed as their white knight in shining armor coming to save them from the big, bad bank. If they are a viable prospect without any other backup plan, approaching it from the perspective of what's in it for you, as the investor, will not go very far. The owner needs to know how working with you will benefit them and their situation.

Also, keep in mind many people in these situations are embarrassed to admit it or downright angry in feeling like they are being taken advantage of. It is not uncommon for someone in foreclosure to deny it or play stupid. They may curse you out and see you as just another person trying to separate them from their assets. For those reasons, I always start the conversation by letting them know my information may not be accurate, but court records indicate they may be in trouble. This affords me the opportunity of advising them what document I saw, and when and where it was filed, so they can reach out to their mortgage company and investigate it. This is the beginning of a relationship where you are now viewed as more of a trusted advisor than a ruthless investor. Wait about two weeks and check the system again to see if the filing has been dismissed, and if it hasn't, give them a call back to play stupid while seeing how their conversation with the bank went.

No matter the outcome of the call to any potential seller, every person you have a conversation with should be added to your CRM or database for future cultivation, except if they explicitly tell you never to contact them again. Nothing in life stays the same for very long, and that's twice as true in real estate. Just because someone is not ready to sell today does not mean they won't be ready next month, next year, or a few years down the road. Staying in touch every few months with a phone call, text, holiday card, or email will keep you at the forefront of their minds. A handwritten letter will also go a long way to separate you from every other investor harassing them. It's also not just their deal you stand to gain; they may know people with real estate-related needs they can refer you to as well.

Real estate is not always a zero-sum game, meaning there does not have to be a party that loses in order for another to make money, but when it comes to distressed deals, this is exactly the opposite. The homeowner stands to lose a great deal in each of these scenarios, which is not your fault. Many will have already made their peace with

66

the loss and are now focusing on how to minimize the damage. These are the conversations you should be having. No one needs to know what the numbers look like on your side or feel strong-armed into making a deal. Take the time to know your prospective seller, understand what the numbers look like for them, and find a way to make it work. The difference between negotiating a successful deal and letting the bank take ownership could just boil down to you helping the person move or staying at no cost for a few weeks while they make other living arrangements. Creativity will serve you well when coupled with compassion and empathy.

"If you don't own a home, buy one. If you own a home, buy another one. If you own two homes buy a third. And lend your relatives the money to buy a home."

— John Paulson

Chapter 4: Buying a Home

Homeownership is supposed to be the American dream, but at times, it can feel more like an American nightmare. Unless you have the luxury of building a home from the ground up, there are undoubtedly concessions you will have to make along the way. Even new construction does not guarantee you will be able to get every feature and dimension included in your dream home. Budget, location, and practicality all play a part in what is or is not possible. The good news is, almost anything can be changed or improved over time. Everything, with the exception of location.

Whether you are a first-time home buyer, upsizing or downsizing your current residence, or looking to get into real estate investing, the chapter will cover all the key information one should be aware of. Markets, laws, and trends are constantly changing. What worked yesterday might not work today, what worked in an urban location might not work in the suburbs, and so on. Many people are quick to give blind advice to others using only their singular experience because they now consider themselves to be experts. Do not fall into that trap. Not everything in this chapter will be relevant to everyone in every situation, so take what you need and leave the rest.

Overview

When it comes to buying a home, there are so many moving pieces involved in the purchasing process. Though we are going to cover these aspects in detail throughout the chapter, it is helpful to have a general overview of everything involved from the time you find a house you love up to the moment you get the keys. The first step in the process is to make an offer in writing to the seller, detailing the terms you are proposing. If working with a realtor, they will do this for you in accordance with local custom, but if you are representing yourself, a simple email containing each of the following components will suffice:

- Price
- Proposed method of financing
- Down payment amount
- Estimated time to close
- Any contingencies
- Your attorney information (in an attorney state)

Once an offer is accepted, contracts are created. This process varies between attorney states and non-attorney states. In an attorney state, the seller's lawyer creates the contract and sends it to the buyer's attorney, who then reviews the terms with their client. In non-attorney states, the buyer's real estate agent creates the contract in the form of a formal offer, which the buyer will sign if both parties are in agreement on all the terms.

If a home inspection was agreed upon, it can happen at three different points, depending on the preferences of the parties involved. Some sellers do not want to have contracts sent out until after the inspection is completed, just in case an issue arises. In many cases, the contracts will be sent out after the inspection has been scheduled. The least likely situation would be to conduct the inspection after contracts are signed as the buyer now loses some leverage in negotiations if issues arise as a result of the inspection.

The next stage of the process is where contracts are signed by both parties and the downpayment is delivered to the seller's attorney or escrow agent. No contract is legally binding until the funds have been received. These funds sit in a designated account until closing, at which point the seller's attorney will disburse them to the seller.

After the contract signing, the bank orders an appraisal to determine the value of the home. This can take anywhere from a few days to a few weeks, depending on the demand and availability of appraisers at the time. The appraiser will need access to the home so they can ascertain the condition in comparison to other recent home sales within a certain radius to make sure they are providing the most accurate estimation of value. The appraisal is then sent to the banker and the buyer.

Then, the title company delivers their report to the buyer's attorney and the bank. If issues have been found, the seller will need to clear them up before the deal can proceed. If everything is in good order, the deal continues to the next stage. Once the title report has been deemed acceptable, the bank conducts a final verification on the credit and income status of the borrower(s), reviews the appraisal, and issues a loan commitment.

With the bank fully ready to proceed, the buyers, sellers, and attorneys or title agents schedule a date for closing. Prior to signing any closing documents, the buyer conducts a final "walkthrough" of the property to ensure the house is being delivered in the expected condition. This will likely mean confirming all appliances work, the mechanical systems are functioning, no damage not previously identified exists, and all furniture and personal items have been removed.

Considerations

Location should be everyone's top concern. What specifically about the location is important will vary from person to person, and this applies to whether it is a first-time home purchase you are going to live in or an investment property you plan to rent to others. Location is also one of those gray areas in real estate where your agent is not allowed to be as open and honest about certain things as they might like to be and you wish they could be. In fact, most buyers do not realize it is against the code of ethics to offer their opinions on certain matters due to federal regulations.

School districts might come as one of the most surprising. Anyone with children generally wants to live in an area where the schools are above average, if not exceptional. After all, school taxes do comprise the largest portion of the property tax bill. It is not uncommon to have two comparable homes with similar taxes in different school districts. One homeowner can send their kids to a top-rated school while the other can be left with an inferior option or forced to shell out for private school tuition. No, that is not an exaggeration. At the time of writing this, my family lives in one of the wealthiest counties in the country, but our local school district leaves much to be desired.

With so many potential pitfalls in where a home is located, why can't agents give you the inside scoop? It comes down to fears of discrimination. The powers that be do not want real estate agents making the determination of what is a "good" school district and what is not. The most they can do is refer you to websites and resources where independent data on school districts is published so you can make your own informed decision. This also applies to asking about how safe a particular area is or what the crime is like. Even if you are looking in the worst neighborhood in the world, where people are shot down on the sidewalks daily, your agent can only refer you to the publicized crime numbers and not insert any opinions.

Neighbors are worth taking into account as well. If you've ever lived in an apartment building where the walls are thin and you potentially have neighbors above, below, and to both sides, then you already know how impactful having a bad neighbor can be on your quality of life. Granted, discerning the quality of your neighbors may not be the easiest thing to do since no one is spending more than an hour or two across a few visits to really get a handle on it, but you can make it a point of going back at different times and on varying days to see if the neighborhood still looks the same. I have always advised people to come back after dark if the first time they saw it was during the day and to swing by on a weekend if a weekday was the last viewing. You would be amazed at how different something can look when more people are out and about – in both good and bad ways.

Having a long-term vision in mind is important as well. Just because a particular neighborhood suits your needs today does not mean it will continue to do so five years from now. A good example of this would be buying a house on a quiet block with a plot of vacant land next door. In the present, having no neighbors provides additional peace and tranquility, but what happens when a developer buys the land and builds a monstrosity on it that obstructs your view or blocks out the sun? Situations like this likely will not be a common occurrence, but they are still worth being aware of.

As you can see, there are plenty of places in the home buyer journey where it is very much "buyer beware," and the misconception that working with a realtor will absolve you of any research only stands to create potential problems. A good friend of mine almost bought a house without knowing this and became distraught when he learned his realtor was under no obligation to disclose another key piece of information. It is your responsibility to check the sex offender registry and make sure there are none living in the area. Even if one happens to be right next door and everyone else is aware of it, it falls under the umbrella of "buyer beware." The same goes for any potentially unappealing facts about the house, including but not limited to a previous owner who died inside, a violent crime being committed there, or a place that is potentially haunted. No one has to disclose any of it.

I know I said earlier just about anything except location could be changed, and for the most part, that is true. However, it is also important to realize any modifications will come at the expense of time, money, or both. Not all renovation projects are created equal, and it would be wise not to start planning your dream home renovation without some professional advice. I've watched countless times as young, inexperienced homebuyers walk through a house for the first time, pointing out all the walls they would knock down and places they would add bathrooms among countless other structural changes. Please do not do this.

You cannot just move a wall. Depending on the construction of the house, some walls are load-bearing, which means they are structurally integral. Without them, the house will literally fall down. There are also plumbing pipes, electrical wires, and other mechanical components inside walls that need to be accounted for before snapping your fingers and overhauling the whole place. In order to do this the right way, an architect or engineer will be needed to assess the situation and provide building plans showing how it can be accomplished. Unless you have an architect or engineer in the family, chances are you will not know whether or not your vision is possible or affordable until after you have moved in. The good news is, there are a few things you can do to prepare in advance.

The first, most straightforward, and prudent option would be to ensure you can live with the house in its current state, just in case there are no viable options. Having a wish list of changes you would like but could live without will make you more confident in your decision and not leave you at risk of wanting to sell the place shortly after buying it. There are some situations where reaching a compromise won't be possible, and it is better to keep looking. If you need three bedrooms but the home you love only has two, or you want gas heat but the current system is oil-fueled, the complexity of the changes could render the house unsuitable for your needs.

The next option would be to ask your home inspector as many questions as possible. While not all home inspectors are contractors or mechanics, they do have extensive knowledge of home construction and can give you off-the-record advice as to what may be feasible and what likely won't. Even if the home is brand new construction and even if you don't plan on changing anything, always pay for the home inspection. Depending on the size of the house and where in the country it is located, most inspections range from five hundred to a thousand dollars, and it will be the best money you ever spent. Skipping a home inspection is like buying a used car without having a mechanic look at it. The deal may seem great at the moment, but the future expenses arising from faulty mechanical systems, structural issues, and any other complex repairs can run tens of thousands of dollars.

Another option I have suggested to some of my more *discerning* clients is to bring a contractor with them when home shopping or, at the very least, before making an offer. If you have one in the family who is willing to do it for free, that would be ideal, but it is not the worst decision in the world to pay someone for their time and expertise to give you their opinion on what can be done and rough estimates of cost. By doing this, you will be in a stronger position when making an offer because you already have some idea of how much additional money needs to be budgeted beyond just the purchase price.

Offers

You did it! After looking through dozens of houses, if not more, you finally found the one you want to make an offer on. So, what happens next? Hopefully, you are working with a licensed real estate professional to assist with the negotiations – and I don't just say that because I am one. There are a lot of emotions involved in buying a home, and any one of them can cause you to make a very costly mistake. Beyond that, sellers do not take unrepresented buyers as seriously as they do those with agents. Now, the one caveat there is the listing agent, who would be thrilled to represent both you and the seller so they can collect double the commission. While there is nothing illegal about representing both sides so long as it is disclosed, I always question how anyone can split their loyalty between both sides in the transaction. At the end of the day, that agent was working with the seller first and will likely lean toward their best interests.

Now, let's think about your offer. Market conditions change on a regular basis, and it would be foolish to think that what worked in a buyer's market in a rural town in middle America would work in a seller's market in a major city. The one factor that does stay the same though is your commitment and desire to make the house yours. If this truly is the forever home you have been dreaming about, it would be wise to remove any thoughts of strong-arm negotiating from your arsenal when making an initial offer. It only takes a minute for the contract to get awarded to a more motivated buyer, so your first offer could very well be your last.

For the sake of this book, we are going to assume it is a home you don't want to lose in a relatively competitive market. The first thing you need to realize is that price alone is not always the deciding factor for a seller. Offers have varying degrees of strength based on the terms they come with. I have seen many deals go to an offer that was not the highest because the offer was appealing to the seller in other ways. Now, that's not to say you will be able to get the seller to take your offer if you are the lowest by a significant margin just because you have other things going in your favor – most commonly the type of financing you will use to close the deal, how quickly you can close, and whether or not you are willing to waive the inspection and/or appraisal.

Even though I said it's not all about price, let's start with the topic of money. We covered multiple options in Chapter 2, all of which boil down to three tiers in the seller's mind. You have your all-cash option, the mortgage option, and the least desirable option of asking them to finance part of the deal. Cash is fairly straightforward, and as the saying goes, "Cash is king." When you have the luxury of paying with your own money instead of getting a bank involved, the strength of your offer is second to none. A seller knows with confidence that as soon as you sign a contract and provide a down payment, there is no way the deal can fall apart. Sure, you can always try to get out of the contract for one reason or another, but generally, with a cash offer, you will be forfeiting your down payment. This peace of mind for the seller will often lead them to accept a *slightly* lower offer than from a buyer who is looking to get a mortgage.

Since most people will need a mortgage of some kind, it is important to know that the different types are not considered equal in the eyes of a seller and their realtor. Here is the list of each option ranked in order of strongest to weakest and the reasons why:

- Conventional with 20% or more down payment: There are several reasons this is considered the gold standard in mortgages. First, the large down payment (even here, cash is king) demonstrates a commitment and shows financial health. Second, the underwriting process and appraisal criteria are the least stringent of all mortgage options. Lastly, they have been around the longest and make people the most comfortable.

- Conventional with less than 20% down payment: The underwriting and appraisal criteria are still relatively lax compared to the next options, but the reduced amount of "skin in the game" can make some sellers wary of your commitment and financial health.
- FHA loans: These loans allow for as little as 3.5% down. If the low cash requirement wasn't enough to scare a seller, the underwriting and appraisal process can become a downright nightmare. FHA appraisers will look for any little thing wrong with the property and not allow the loan to close unless the seller makes the necessary repairs prior to closing, and no seller really wants to deal with that if they have a better option on the table.
- VA loans: It is a shame VA loans rank dead last on the list, but they are notoriously difficult to close, their appraisers make FHA inspections look like a walk in the park, and it can drag on for months before closing.

Regardless of how you make your offer, remember the emotions we spoke about earlier and how they can set you up for a costly mistake. Well, the seller has emotions too. You are talking about a home they likely lived in for many years, where they created memories, raised a family, and so many other intangible events you can not quantify. For those reasons, sellers can be easily insulted when someone offers them far less than their asking price. This can result in them not only rejecting your offer outright but also not giving you the opportunity to renegotiate, even if you were willing to come up substantially.

Think I'm kidding? I had two separate clients in completely different scenarios who did not follow my advice and decided to make what the sellers deemed to be offensive offers. We'll call the first client Paul to protect his identity. He absolutely fell in love with a one-of-a-kind brick home listed at $1.1M. Now, Paul was a savvy real estate investor, who already owned several homes in this neighborhood and thought he knew his way around a negotiating table. In his mind, the home was not worth more than $900K. On paper, he may have been right, but he demanded I start the negotiations at $875K despite my advice. He felt he would have the upper hand because he was making an all-cash offer. What Paul failed to incorporate into his strategy is that he was buying the house for his daughter and grandkids to live in, not as a straight investment property like the rest of his portfolio.

As it turned out, the seller designed and built this house herself. It was like her child. When her agent presented the offer, she went ballistic – insulted was an understatement. While she did not end the negotiations there, she did counter with a price of $1.15M – higher than the original asking price. Paul thought she was playing games and would ultimately come around. She was not, and she did not. They continued to show the home and ultimately received several other offers above the asking price. Paul, knowing he was never going to let this house go, pleaded with me to help him get an offer accepted. The happy ending here is that Paul did wind up buying the house but for $200K more than asking and, in my opinion, at least $300K more than he would have paid if he simply made a reasonable offer upfront before other people had a chance to drive the price up.

Then, we have Armando. Armando was another well-seasoned real estate investor with more property than even he can probably count. He was looking to help a key employee purchase her first home, and she was madly in love with a condo overlooking the water. Unlike Paul's house, this one had been on the market for quite some time and did not appear to be getting a lot of traction. Listed at $450K, it was definitely overpriced slightly, but the market was hot and supply was low. When Armando told me to submit an offer of $300K (33% less than asking), I asked if I heard him correctly, thinking for sure he must have meant $400K. He was resolute in operating the way he did for all of his investments since he was also offering all-cash terms, and I wish I could say this story had a happy ending. Our seller here was so insulted she had her agent tell me she would not sell to us under any circumstances. If she had to take it off the market and not sell, then that was what she would do. And, that's exactly what she did. To this day, over a year later, it remains unsold, and when I periodically check in with the listing agent to ask if we can make a higher offer, I am told she will not sell to my client.

Hopefully, there is something to be learned from these two gentlemen who thought their experience and cash offers would outweigh a seller's emotions. Most people will not be in either of their situations though because all-cash purchases are not the norm. The median home price in the United States just passed $400K for the first time ever, and even if you had that much money lying around, chances are, you would prefer to let the bank step in and finance as much of it as possible.

There is also more to an offer than just the type of financing, let's move on to some of the other contingencies you can put in your offer. Sellers want to have the smoothest possible experience, and each additional uncertainty for them to worry about can wind up getting your offer passed over for someone who appears easier to deal with. One of the biggest stumbling blocks in this regard is the home inspection. I know I told you never to skip one, so don't misconstrue this. A good home inspector is there to write up anything and everything they discover to protect you as their client and their own professional reputation. Many of these items will be nothing more than cosmetic, but some could range into more serious territory.

How can you get the peace of mind of conducting a home inspection without unwittingly pushing the seller toward another offer where they waived the inspection process? Luckily for my clients, and anyone reading this book, there are two clever ways to get around this. To be clear though, neither of these strategies is likely to help you renegotiate the price of the house. What they will provide is an overall exit strategy should you find any major issues that would preclude you from carrying through with the transaction. In a perfect world, the seller will accept your offer with an inspection contingency in place, but we all know this is far from a perfect world, and every advantage in a competitive market is welcomed.

The first option would be to conduct your inspection without the seller ever knowing it is happening. Before you think I'm crazy or up to no good, let me assure you there are ways to do this on the straight and narrow. The first way, as mentioned earlier, would be bringing an inspector or contractor along with you on one of the viewings before ever submitting your offer. Doing this will give you a leg up on anyone else who may want to do theirs after the fact. Another clever, albeit slightly duplicitous, approach would be to ask to go back and take measurements for furniture. Once you are granted access, you can bring along your inspector or contractor to conduct the informal inspection.

If you want to make the formal request for an inspection, without it being held against you, my next piece of advice would be to frame it for "informational purposes only." The wording of this tells the seller you will not attempt to renegotiate the contract price. You are conducting the inspection for your own knowledge in budgeting for what might need to be repaired after closing. Many times, this request will only be granted if you agree to sign the purchase contract before conducting the inspection, which eliminates your ability to back out without needing to find another escape clause.

The reason I say all these options are above board is that you will have no legal recourse to use any of the findings against the seller in an attempted renegotiation. Should something of monumental concern come up on one of these inspections, you can and should bring it to the attention of the seller's team. While they are not obliged to make any concessions, it never hurts to ask. There is always the chance they will be equally surprised by the findings and agree to remedy it or grant a price concession to keep the process moving. It is uncommon, but I have witnessed it work on several occasions.

The next thing you can do to make your offer appear stronger is not for the faint of heart, and I do not recommend attempting it unless you have substantial cash reserves or a lender who will help you out if things don't go in your favor. Offering to waive your appraisal as a contingency is kind of a misnomer since your bank will not actually let you waive it. They conduct an appraisal for their own protection, ensuring the home is worth the amount of money they will be lending on it. Normally, if a home does not appraise for the agreed-upon sales amount or higher, the bank will not go forward with the transaction unless one of two things happens: the sale price gets reduced to the appraised value or the buyer makes up the difference with their own cash. So long as the buyer has not waived their appraisal, the seller generally has no recourse but to lower the price or walk away from the deal entirely.

When you waive your appraisal, you are basically telling the seller up front that, in the event the house appraises for less than the purchase price, you will pay the difference in cash so the transaction can continue. While the chances of an appraisal coming in significantly lower than expected are low, I have seen it happen and will not understate the risk. Because this is no longer a contingency in the contract, the seller is within their rights to keep your down payment if you can't or won't shell out the money needed to cover the difference. The loophole here is still having your overall mortgage contingency intact. This means that if your loan is declined for any other reason outside of the appraisal, you can get off the hook and out of the transaction with your down payment in hand. Whenever I employ this strategy, I make sure the loan officer is fully aware of what we are doing and have their agreement up front to help get the loan declined for some other reason in the event the appraisal backfires.

Please note that many of the strategies presented above can be complex and emotionally taxing to navigate on your own. If you find yourself in a situation where you are thinking of employing one or several of them, it is highly advisable to consult with a real estate professional first. Many states require you to have an attorney as part of the transaction, and if that is applicable in your situation, then they would be the best person to consult. Your real estate agent or broker should also have a fairly good idea of how to navigate each eventuality in such a way that your offer comes across as strong as possible while also leaving you room for protection in the event something doesn't go according to plan.

You should also plan for a drawn-out negotiation process with periods of give and take. While it can be frustrating, any kind of dialogue with the selling side is a positive sign and opens the door for negotiations.

Negotiations

After successfully navigating the offer process, you might find yourself in a position where negotiations are necessary. It's very rare for the first offer to be accepted exactly as presented unless you come in excessively high over the asking price or some other obscure circumstance exists. Making a decent first offer and having the seller come back with a different price is perfectly normal. It is human nature to want to get the best possible deal. That's why people haggle prices on everything from cars and professional services to homes and salaries.

Just because you earned the right to negotiate does not mean you should lose sight of the ultimate goal of purchasing the house. This is where it becomes incredibly important to understand your "why" and know how badly you want the specific house in question. If your "why" is simply to get the best price compared to what they were asking for and you are willing to go through one failed negotiation after another, then, by all means, lowball and play hardball all day long. But if this really is the house for you, take a step back and think about what your unrealized cost would be if the contract is awarded to someone who negotiated better.

- Would you need to keep renting?
- Will your creditworthiness change in the near future?
- Can you find a similar house you like as much in an acceptable time frame?
- Do you have any upcoming changes in employment?
- Is your family outgrowing the present space?

These are just a few of the questions it is impossible to assign a monetary value to and just a few of the ones you should be asking yourself before entering into negotiations. You are not buying a car that depreciates and has countless identical options from other sellers. You are not negotiating the price of a new roof in a major city where there are numerous qualified contractors you can fall back on if talks go sideways. You are buying the largest asset of your life, where you will likely live a significant portion of your life, raise a family, and create memories. The few thousand dollars you might save may never add up to the opportunity you lose.

That's not to say you should throw money out the window though. It is a common pricing strategy in many industries, real estate included, to start with a much higher number than is reasonable knowing that potential buyers will try to negotiate the price down. If a seller is looking for a certain number, they are likely to list the price at $10K, $20K, or even $50K over what they would be happy with. This way, when a seller comes along and offers them anything under the inflated asking price but over the number they were looking for, the deal is already a winner for them.

Knowing games are played on both sides of the transaction when it comes to securing the best price, it is important to keep control of your emotions. Negotiating the price of anything is similar to playing poker – a house just happens to be a very high-stakes game with only two players. Yes, there is always the good cop/bad cop approach where a spouse, sibling, or other interested party may have differing opinions on the best outcome, but generally, the buying side and selling side are the two main players at the table. No one has ever won a poker game by letting on to just how good their hand was, but bad hands get bluffed into good ones all the time.

So, what's the bluff in a real estate negotiation? Depending on how many other people are bidding on the house, the bluff is generally the prospect walking away from the table. When many other parties have offers submitted, this option won't work so well, but if you are the only offer, the seller may be hard-pressed to go back to the drawing board and wait for a new buyer to come along. Just like in poker though, there is always the chance someone calls your bluff. In poker, you lose the hand and hopefully have enough chips left to fight another round. In real estate, the outcome of a failed bluff is not so cut and dry,

Sure, you can follow through and turn the bluff into a reality by walking away if you can live without getting the house, but the minute you bluff walking away and the seller ceases negotiations, your hand has weakened considerably. When someone goes from walking away back to making counteroffers, everyone knows you had no intention of walking away to begin with. In these situations, you are less likely to get the seller to come down in price as much as they might have if you used a different tactic. In fact, they may not come down at all assuming you will now do whatever it takes to stay in the game.

Don't let all the prior talk about price lead you to believe money is the only negotiable component in a real estate transaction. It is the most common and where the majority of the focus is placed, but there are also other areas where negotiations are acceptable and may be viewed as more reasonable or acceptable to the seller. Believe it or not, almost anything can be negotiable, and this list of other items you can try getting the seller to throw in is not meant to be all-inclusive:

- Furniture
- Inspection fee
- Closing date
- Seller's concession toward closing costs
- Collectibles
- Fitness equipment
- Outdoor living items

Don't forget all the contingencies we spoke about in the section on Offers either. Any of those items can also be used to strengthen your negotiating position by giving up something you can live without instead of trying to offer something you don't have. Maybe the buyer and seller are at an impasse over $20K on the purchase price. If the buyer is already at the maximum end of their budget and physically cannot go any higher, they may decide waiving their home inspection would make their lower offer more favorable. The same could work in reverse as well if the buyer has more room in their budget. Now they can hold tight to the contingency of an inspection but offer more money instead (and potentially use the results of the inspection to renegotiate a better price if significant issues are uncovered).

While there is no saying whether a seller will be agreeable to any or all of your negotiation requests, the only guarantee is you will never get anything you don't ask for. As long as you handle the request with respect, the worst someone can say is "no." We take hearing that word for granted numerous times a day without ever batting an eye, so don't hold back asking for something on the biggest purchase of your life. You might just wind up pleasantly surprised.

Team Dynamics

They say there is no "I" in the word team. While that is true, there is no "I" in real estate either. You may be the prospective buyer, and, as such, one of the most important people in the transaction, but you cannot do it alone. In most states, it would actually be considered a huge conflict of interest to try handling all aspects of a single real estate transaction. Each deal is unique, and the more emotionally attached or involved you are, the easier it is to exercise poor judgment. In any given transaction, you may be working with an inspector, two real estate agents, a lender, an appraiser, as many as three attorneys, a title company, and an insurance agent. With that many specialized professions, the risks of head-butting and professional cockiness runs high.

Let's start with the home inspector. This should be one of the easiest people on the team to deal with, and if you are the prospective buyer, this is absolutely someone you should primarily speak directly with instead of using a third party. Even if the inspector comes recommended by your realtor and the realtor handles the scheduling of the appointment, be as involved as possible. The most important thing to remember here is the inspector works for you, the buyer, and not the realtor. It does not matter if a realtor refers a ton of business to them or not; their job is to tell you the good, the bad, and the ugly without concern for whether the deal closes or not. If, at any time, you get the impression this is not the case, consider finding your own inspector – and possibly finding a new realtor!

Do not let the inspection happen without being physically present, so the inspector can walk you through their findings instead of waiting until you are overwhelmed with a 50-100 page report. Most of the issues they note are generally nowhere near as bad as they might seem, and having firsthand experience with them can go a long way for peace of mind and deciding how to tackle them. Again, always confirm upfront that the inspector is working for you and in your best interest. Even though their legal responsibility is to you and not the realtor, who gives them a lot of business, it never hurts to let them know upfront that you are also aware of this.

The two real estate agents might sound self-explanatory, but one is there to represent you, and the other represents the seller. The only exception would be an agent who is representing both sides, which we mentioned earlier is not technically illegal, but we will discuss this further in Chapter 9. In a perfect world, the buyer should never speak with the seller or their agent, and vice versa. The agents are the mediators on the transaction and handle all communications between their clients to ensure the process runs smoothly and key information is not getting lost in translation during a game of telephone. For the duration of the transaction, the buyer's agent will wear many hats; everything from therapist to coach – even occasionally a real estate professional. That might sound like a bad joke but once a house is under contract, most of the work does shift away from real estate facts and figures and moves toward hand-holding, managing emotions and expectations.

The lender is the person securing your financing for the purchase. They could either work directly for a bank or lender or work with several different lenders. Regardless of which, their function is the same, and it is time-sensitive. It is advisable to authorize them to communicate with the buyer's real estate agent so they can coordinate matters that don't require the buyer's time, but most of the contact will be directly between the broker and the buyer. The buyer will need to provide all requested documents to the mortgage broker in a timely fashion and work through any potential financial issues that may prevent approval.

The appraiser is hired by the mortgage lender to make sure the home is worth what the sales price states because it is the lender's money on the line in the event you default. But just because they are hired by the bank does not mean the lender has much communication with them. In fact, they are not allowed to contact the appraiser directly, as it can be viewed as a way to influence the valuation. Generally, the lender will provide the listing agent's contact information to schedule access to the home, at which time the listing agent will coordinate with the buyer's agent to allow the appraiser access. This is more of an accepted entitlement in certain markets where sellers' agents feel the appraisal is for the buyer, and therefore, their agent should do the work.

The three attorneys are where the process can get fun, which really means bogged down. There is a saying in real estate that "attorneys kill deals." While there are many great attorneys out there who bend over backward to make deals work instead of killing them, there are many more who do the bare minimum or actively try to make the situation more difficult than it needs to be. One attorney works for the seller and prepares the sales contract. The second attorney works for the buyer and reviews the contract with them to request any changes that may be needed, and the third attorney works for the lender and will not get involved until it is time to schedule a closing. From experience, it is safe to say having solid communication between attorneys and real estate agents will ensure minor issues can get handled before they become monumental.

The title company is responsible for providing "insurance" on the title of the home. This entails certifying the person selling the home is the actual owner with the authority to do so. They will also search public records to make sure there are no property line disputes, unpaid taxes, or any other undisclosed liens that could leave the new owner in a precarious situation down the road. In attorney states, the title is ordered by the buyer's attorney (generally someone they have an established relationship with), and the attorney is the only one communicating with them. However, a preferred way of handling the title would be for the buyer and their agent to be in agreement with who is used (the buyer is paying for the service after all) and make it known they want to be able to communicate directly with the title agent to ensure any potential issues are dealt with promptly.

Last, but not least, is the insurance agent who will be providing the homeowner's insurance policy. Too many times, this part of the transaction is an oversight, and buyers are left scrambling a few days prior to closing in search of an insurance policy. There are literally thousands of insurance companies capable of issuing these policies, all at different costs, levels of coverage, and varying qualities of service. Having to make a last-minute decision to get a policy in place for an upcoming closing is likely to leave the buyer overpaying and underinsured, so the buyer and their agent should start shopping policies early on in the process to avoid this situation and to rest assured the premium is not going to adversely affect their mortgage approval status.

If it seems like an awful lot of people are involved in one transaction, there can be, especially when there is no clearly outlined plan for how everyone is going to work together. No matter which role you play in a transaction, always make it a point to find out early on who else will be involved in the joint effort. Get their contact information and establish upfront who is authorized to speak with whom and what the expectations are for the forms of communication and anticipated reply times. A little extra work at the beginning of the process will save a lot of time and headaches in the long run.

Sometimes, team members may come in the most unusual forms, even as the seller's real estate agent – or the sellers themselves. This is when real estate can be both profitable and rewarding. It also pays to love what you do, so there is never a question about going above and beyond to make the magic happen for clients. I was introduced to a ninety-year-old woman who was thinking about selling the home she had lived in for the last 50+ years, as it was more house than she needed and the upkeep was becoming more trouble than it was worth. These can always be challenging situations because of the emotional attachment, but also from the shock that comes with having tons of strangers traipsing through your home, judging with their eyes and snide comments. After running some numbers with the sellers, I determined what number would make them happy and was able to match it to a repeat buyer of mine without having to hold a single open house.

Every part of the transaction went so smoothly, the owner and her daughter referred me to their neighbors across the street who had a similar situation, where we were able to do the exact same thing for them. But in the interim, my original client was now living with her daughter in a tiny one-bedroom apartment on the fifth floor. Not an ideal living arrangement to say the least, but even less so when it drags on for almost a year. Ultimately, they could not take it anymore and re-engaged my assistance – this time to help them find a two-bedroom condo they could move to. They really didn't know exactly what they wanted, just a general idea of the area and price range based on the cash they still had from the home sale.

These types of situations, even with clients who already love you, can be very challenging. With such vague criteria in such a wide search area, the potential for spending hours running around and suffering disappointment was too real. That was part of what we experienced in the first two weeks. Nothing could quite live up to the memories of the home they sold, and the condos they did like often lacked a particular feature our elderly client needed. That was until the day we opened the door to a beautiful townhome in a riverfront complex. As soon as I stepped inside, my jaw hit the floor – to the point where the clients asked me if something was wrong with the unit. My response was, "The only thing wrong is that you don't live here."

From the entranceway, you could already experience the panoramic view of the river off the living room balcony. After only taking a few steps inside, those views continued across the master bedroom. My client then sat on the balcony in her wheelchair, enchanted by the water. Her daughter agreed with my earlier assertion and told me to make it happen. When I confirmed with her mom that this was what she wanted to do, my heart broke as she said to me, "I would be happy dying here. I've worked my entire life and have never had a new kitchen, a new bathroom, or a view. This has it all."

But we were not out of the woods yet. Needless to say, with those kinds of views in a newly renovated unit, there would be stiff competition. My client's daughter asked if we could negotiate a price below asking because they were all-cash buyers, and as we have heard many times in this book, I explained why that would not be a good idea. "Would you be ok with someone else getting this instead of you because they offered $20K more?" I asked her.

"I wouldn't be able to live with myself," was her answer.

So, I got to work. I called the listing agent from the car to let her know we would be making an offer and to confirm there were other offers – confirming my suspicions there were multiple over-asking. I went straight back to the office to draft my offer letter along with a heartwarming note in the email about my client. At around 10 PM, I awoke (which is a miracle in itself because I sleep like a dead man) to a text message from the listing agent saying our offer would not be accepted because we did not have enough cash. Apparently, she overlooked the fact that there were two bank statements attached to my offer, which combined had more than sufficient funds. Her last message said, "It's too late. The owners will make a decision in the morning based on the facts I presented to them."

I was wide awake now and unwilling to accept that my client's fate would be subjected to a technicality. I immediately typed a book of a reply where I quoted my client directly about being happy dying in the house and how much it would mean to her along with a picture (so glad I took one) of my client on the balcony in her wheelchair smiling. This has a low percentage success rate since most sellers are more concerned with profits than people, but I was pulling out every trick in my book. The next morning, the agent called me to say we were not the highest offer, nor were we the highest all-cash offer, but after she read my message to her clients, they decided we were the only possible choice. Turns out, it was an estate sale. Their parents had both recently passed away within weeks of one another, and they remembered how much they loved the unit and wanted it to go to someone who would get as much joy out of it as they did.

To this day, I still tear up thinking about how happy everyone was in this transaction. There was hugging, crying, and pictures being taken at the closing table. I'm pretty sure even the lawyers cried. The moral of this story has nothing to do with how great I am though because it all depended on my clients accepting my advice to offer more than they wanted, the listing agent having enough heart to share my client's story, and the sellers taking a step back to think about more than money. It is so rare for all those stars to align, but when they do, it is magical and makes everything else worthwhile.

Trust but Verify

Trust is one of the interesting interpersonal dynamics. Some of us are far too trusting and would believe anything we are told, and others are eternal skeptics who won't believe anything without seeing and touching it. But the large majority fall somewhere in between the two. We trust those who we think have our best interests at heart like family, friends, and paid professionals to name a few. Yet too often we find the ones we trusted the most to be the ones who cause us the most harm through incompetence, unprofessionalism, or outright dereliction of duty. When it comes to purchasing real estate, the stakes are just too high not to verify certain details of the transaction.

Depending on the location, property taxes can be one of the most significant ongoing expenses of owning real estate and also one of the most commonly overlooked. No one should ever purchase property without first contacting the local tax assessor's office to not only confirm the current taxes but also to inquire as to when, if any, reassessments may be scheduled. Every popular real estate website will tell you what the property taxes are for a property, so you may be wondering why you should take the time to investigate. Let's take a look at a couple of scenarios to see what could possibly go wrong with accepting what the internet says.

In the case of an FSBO, the tax information you see listed on sites like Zillow and Realtor.com was input by the seller. This can be problematic for several reasons. The first is because the website does not check for accuracy. Not to say a seller is intentionally being deceptive, but they may not even be aware of what their actual tax bill is after combining county, city, and school taxes, so they simply plug in an estimated number. The current owner may also benefit from certain tax benefits like the STAR or enhanced STAR programs, which are not transferable to the new owner unless they qualify. The second reason is due to the reassessments mentioned earlier. What might be the current tax amount due at listing could change in the next 12 months, and the seller may either not be aware of it or choose not to disclose that information.

The most common real estate listing involves a real estate agent entering the property information into the multiple listing service (MLS), which feeds the information over to each of the sites we already mentioned. Though there are some good agents who will verify the information, most agents merely accept what the seller tells them the taxes are. This leaves you in the same situation as if the seller listed it themselves and still leaves you no recourse if discrepancies are detected after closing. No one wants to get their first tax bill only to find out it is substantially higher than anticipated.

In the case of off-market deals, where the buyer might be an investor or homeowner searching for creative deals, public websites like Zillow or paid membership sites like Remine or Propstream are used to estimate the property value and tax information. This value is sourced by scrubbing the internet for historical data on the property. Not all tax assessors make their valuation tables or assessment rates available online or easy to find, so the likelihood of stumbling on inaccurate information runs high. A deal can go from profitable to negative at the drop of a hat if the tax information is not current and accurate.

The next area to perform your due diligence is Homeowners Association (HOA) fees. These fees are only applicable when purchasing a cooperative apartment (mainly found in NYC and other major metropolitan areas), condominium, townhouse, or home situated in a private community. The problem with HOA fees is they can come in many shapes and sizes, where a seller can easily omit relevant information by accident or on purpose. It is always a good idea to confirm with the HOA management what the total annual dues are, inclusive of any special assessments, one-time additional payments, and extra charges for things like parking spaces and access to certain amenities. It also never hurts to ask if they foresee any changes in the monthly charges or special assessments in the next one to two years so you can budget accordingly.

Insurance is the last major area to pay close attention to. A standard homeowner's policy can run $1K or less, and many lenders will use that number as the basis for qualifying your loan, but there are two reasons never to accept that at face value. For starters, your actual premium could be substantially higher if the neighborhood has a high crime rate, the roof is nearing the end of its useful life, or any other number of factors. The second reason is the biggest factor that can blow your insurance numbers out of the water, and that is flood insurance. As a rule of thumb, anything near a body of water will require flood insurance, but houses in low-lying areas could also be subjected to the requirement. Never accept the seller's assurance of flood insurance not being required just because they don't currently have it. Check with your lender and the Federal Emergency Management Agency (FEMA) website to confirm if this is going to become a problem preventing you from getting to closing.

The time to verify is preferably before ever entering into a purchase contract, but that is not always possible due to time constraints and market demands. There is generally a 30-60 day window from contract signing to closing where all due diligence can be performed, and this is the time any issues should be presented to the seller. Even though contracts have been signed, amendments can be made if material differences are discovered between what was represented at contract signing and what the research uncovers. Considering some of the areas we mentioned can wind up costing tens of thousands of dollars over time, anyone on the buyer's side should be more concerned with protecting their best interests and not offending anyone by double-checking their information to be accurate.

"Buyers decide in the first eight seconds of seeing a home if they're interested in buying it. Get out of your car, walk in their shoes and see what they see within the first eight seconds."

— Barbara Corcoran

Get Real!

Chapter 5: Selling a Home

Selling a home can be more stressful than buying one. As an investor who has sold their fair share of homes, I can attest to that. In fact, even as a licensed real estate broker in three states with dozens of transactions under my belt, I would never represent myself again. Emotions run high and a little bit of knowledge can turn into a dangerous thing when dealing with buyers who have significantly less experience, professionalism, or sincerity. Granted, the feelings will vary based on whether you are selling the home you have lived in or an investment property with little sentimental value, but the strain of managing the process on your own is equally as stressful in either scenario.

Whether you are a homeowner, an investor, or a real estate agent, there are components to this type of real estate transaction you might not have taken into consideration before. "If you build it, they will come," is a famous quote from *Field of Dreams*, but unfortunately, life does not always work that way. Just because you listed the house does not guarantee anyone is going to come or buy it. There are several simple steps a seller can take to ensure they get maximum visibility, minimal liability, and ideally the best price and/or terms. The key is being open-minded to trying something you might not have thought of before, no matter how crazy it might sound.

Negotiations

As a seller, your goal in the negotiation process is the opposite of the buyer's. Where they are trying to get the lowest price or put down the smallest amount of money, the seller is looking to maximize the price paid and get as much money down or contingencies waived as possible. This is why it is important to remember an offer price is nothing more than words on paper until it is substantiated. Too many sellers have tunnel vision about what they think their house is worth and will forgo all offers that don't rise to this mythical level, and they are doing themselves a terrible disservice.

High offer prices are great, but they are not always realistic. As we learned in Chapter 4, if the offer is not all cash, there are many things that can make the process more challenging than it needs to be or outright kill it altogether. If you are in no rush to sell or don't really care one way or another, holding out for the highest price is not the worst strategy. But if you need to be out sooner than later for whatever reason, focus more on what it will take to get the deal done without costing you time or money in the process.

Always remember most all-cash offers will generally be lowball offers because of the security of the offer. These buyers are familiar with the expression "cash is king" and have no problems telling you how many other sellers would kill for their offer. While they may not be wrong, that does not mean they can get away with pushing you around unless you happen to be in a hopeless situation. If someone has enough cash to make an offer at one price, chances are, there is more cash to go higher – if they see a reason to do so.

With this in mind, anyone on the seller's side should balance emotion with strategy. Find out what it is about the house they like so much to prompt their all-cash offer. It might be because of the proximity to relatives, the school district, certain amenities only your house has, or any number of personal factors. The trick is in getting them to verbalize their "why", so you can turn around and use their own words against them when stressing all the reasons they don't want to lose this property. They need to feel you recognize the value of what you have and question whether or not you would really go with a higher, non-cash offer.

Beyond just the price, the same items buyers can push to negotiate can be used in your favor for a quicker closing. It can't hurt to ask for them to waive the inspection or commit to a 30 or 45-day closing. Each additional concession you can get from a non-cash buyer goes a long way to show how committed they are to making the deal work.

Most lawyers don't like it, but I have witnessed deals where the buyer wanted the home so badly they were willing to make a portion of their down payment non-refundable and allow the seller to access it prior to closing so they could have more leverage when making offers on a new home.

It's sometimes easier said than done, but when evaluating potential offers, try to learn as much about the potential buyers as you can and put yourself in their shoes. Taking this approach can often help you see things differently and potentially understand what their motives are, thus helping you figure out who the most serious buyers are. Think about two potential offers with identical terms and conditions. Both have the exact same offer price and financing, and everything is equal except for their underlying motivations for buying this particular property. On the one side is a young family with children who will need to be living there within the next 60 days to get enrolled in their desired public school. On the other hand, there is a young, single real estate investor who plans on using the house as a rental property. Which party do you think is going to take the opportunity more seriously, and do everything in their power to close within the allotted time frame? Sure, there is always the chance it could be the investor, but the more likely choice is the family whose future rides on getting the home.

Revisit your "why" behind selling. That reason is not just limited to reasons like, "I need to move," or "we need more space." Yes, those factors come into play, but there are other considerations as well. Do you have close friends and family members who will still live in the community? If so, would selling to a punk rock band be in their best interest? Nothing against punk rock bands, but the potential for disruption runs high, and the few extra dollars you make on the sale might not be worth the resentment it breeds with those you left behind. If you have fond childhood memories there and want to know that someone else will get the same enjoyment from it, selling to a developer who plans to knock it down might not be the best bet. Truly understanding what the most important thing in the sale is will allow you to hone in more on the offers that align with your other non-monetary objectives. And if the most important thing for you is the money, that is totally okay too.

Always remember, any offer is just that and nothing more – an offer – until a contract is signed. This is where a lot of games get played, especially with all-cash offers. High numbers will get thrown out to keep you focused on their negotiations and ruling out others, but contract signing will not come quickly or easily. Maybe the inspection that was done only for informational purposes is now being leveraged for a price reduction. The buyer might create an issue at the last minute in the hopes of getting you to bend rather than fight when you are so close to getting a deal signed. Whatever it is, make sure there is a realistic expectation of when contracts should be signed and clearly convey you will continue entertaining other offers until the ink dries and the checks clear.

Legality

Caveat emptor, or let the buyer beware, is a time-tested saying society has made acceptable. It basically means we, as consumers, should shoulder the burden of doing our own due diligence before purchasing goods or services, instead of relying on the merchant or provider to be honest and transparent. The same philosophy can hold true when working with real estate transactions, except it is not quite as simple as it sounds.

Let's start with any of the physical defects that could exist in your house. The mechanical and structural integrity of a home is one of the key factors a buyer will be concerned with and part of the reason why home inspections are so important. Most states require the seller to complete some type of property disclosure report prior to entering into a contract. These disclosures vary by state and can run several pages long with questions surrounding everything from the basement to the roof, leaving no stone left unturned.

Certain states, like New York, allow the seller to skip this arduous and potentially expensive process by offering the buyer a $500 credit at closing. Most would agree this is a small price to pay not to start taking all the skeletons out of the closet. In fact, I can count on one hand how many times a seller in New York opted not to give the credit and decided to complete the disclosure instead. This is another area where both a seller and their real estate agent need to exercise an abundance of caution. Offering the credit in no way indicates the seller knows something is wrong with the house, it just offers a way to simplify the process and expedite a closing.

Should a seller opt to voluntarily complete the disclosure or transact in a state where it cannot be waived, it should be done with complete honesty. The questions on these disclosures are worded in such a way as to note whether the seller has "any knowledge" of specific deficiencies such as a leaky roof, faulty water heater, or structural damage, just to name a few. Oftentimes, listing agents will recommend having your own inspection conducted in order to uncover any problems before the buyer finds them or to give peace of mind that none exist. While this can be informative, I would leverage another well-known expression: "Don't ask questions you don't want the answers to." Once you open the door and bring certain issues to light, you can't unsee them. You now have knowledge of any deficiencies noted during that inspection and will be forced to tell the seller or waive the disclosure.

There is a big difference between saying there are no known issues with your roof, even though you know it is old, because you are not experiencing any leaks or other hazardous conditions and actively covering up potential issues. If there are visible leaks on the top floor ceiling of your house, this is now a known issue, so patching and painting to hide signs of the damage and certifying the waiver would be considered fraud. The same could be said for having a roofer assess that you need a new roof and provide a written estimate, then choosing not to disclose that to the buyer. This is where having a pre-sale inspection done on your own home can backfire if you want or are required to fill out the disclosure.

When in doubt, the best practice would be to avoid the disclosure at all costs or answer as honestly as possible. Most times, the items you are noting on the disclosure will be fairly obvious to a buyer anyway and not worth the risk of fraud. A keen eye can tell when a roof looks worn out, mechanical systems all have dates and service records attached, and major structural issues stick out like a sore thumb. If you label the sale "as is," the buyer is put on notice that you acknowledge the house needs work, and it has been priced accordingly. It's not a fool-proof method for ensuring a buyer won't use your disclosure report to try and renegotiate the price, but at least it puts everyone on the same playing field.

Another key legal area that oftentimes comes up during a property sale has to do with modifications to the home. Every municipality is different in their building codes for what requires a permit and what does not. Generally, minor upgrades that do not alter the layout of the house like painting, putting in carpet, and changing light fixtures or appliances will not require a permit anywhere, while more substantial changes like replacing the roof, converting an unfinished basement into living space, and adding rooms – especially kitchens and bathrooms – will. Most sellers do not give this much consideration since they live there and either don't realize they need a permit or willingly choose to avoid getting one.

We could spend an entire chapter on why someone would opt to not get a permit, but it usually boils down to saving time, money, and headaches. The building department charges for permits, takes time to issue them, requires you to use licensed and insured contractors (which means any DIY folks are excluded), and will inspect the finished work before closing out the permit. If you are someone who has done any of these major modifications without a permit, this is the time when it can come back to bite you in the butt. Remember, the title company is going to verify everything about the house, and the appraiser is going to provide the bank with a visual report of what they noted on their visit.

Why does this matter?

If your buyer is paying all cash, it might not matter so much. There will be far less oversight and red tape to cut through on the way to closing. Even if the title company discovers outstanding permit issues or a Certificate of Occupancy that does not match the current condition of the home (such as only two bathrooms instead of three or single-family occupancy instead of two-family occupancy) because a permit was never filed, the transaction can still proceed so long as the buyer does not object. By doing so, they are effectively assuming the liability for any of the permit issues, and it will become their headache down the road when they want to sell. But if the buyer is getting a mortgage, the bank will not allow them to proceed unless the appraiser's description of bedrooms, bathrooms, and kitchens matches what the title company shows on their search. If the title company discovers open permits because a part of the process was not completed properly, the bank will halt the entire process until those issues are resolved.

When making renovation-related decisions, try to look through a long-term lens instead of acting in the short-term best interest. Yes, it can be expensive to file for permits. It can be stressful dealing with the building department and completing the project to the letter of the law. For any substantial increases in your home's value, there will likely be an increase in your property taxes, but if you cut corners to avoid these situations, you are ultimately robbing yourself of the equity you worked so hard to gain. The true appraised value of your home will only reflect what is legally supposed to be there. Even when the buyer and seller both agree the home in its current condition should be worth more, the bank will not care.

Marketing

The expression "selling a home" is always a humorous one. A home, similar to other big-ticket items like cars or boats, cannot be *sold*. It is impossible to sell someone on a purchase that is as expensive as it is personal. Some agents will walk around a house with the potential buyer pointing out the most obvious items like, "Look at the size of this living room," or "The kitchen has stainless steel appliances." Unless the buyer is blind, none of this is helpful in pushing someone toward the point of making a decision. What can be influenced though, is just how many potential buyers decide to come for an in-person tour, which is the first step before any sale can possibly happen.

In order to bring as much traffic into a home as possible, marketing strategies are incredibly important, whether it be an owner trying to sell the house on their own or with the help of a real estate agent. We live in an age where information is at our fingertips every second of the day, and we tend to think we know everything we need to know after researching something online. Therefore, you need to give prospective buyers everything they need to know so the home calls out to those who would be the best fit to buy it.

All marketing starts with great pictures. The average human attention span has been likened to that of a goldfish, or less, so it is going to require something eye-catching to draw people in. It is equal parts art and science to create the perfect balance of pictures that will visually tell the story you want a buyer to experience. Too many pictures of the outside with very few of the inside will leave viewers with the feeling something is wrong inside. The same goes for listings where all pictures are of the interior and none of the exterior. The intent might be to highlight the best features of the home, but in reality, it does more harm than good.

A special note should be made about using professional photography, digitally enhanced images, and virtually staged photographs. There is a fine line between delivering the best possible representation of your home and deceptive advertising. Just like advertisements for restaurants where the food always looks perfect, but then you get there only to find a sloppy mess and instantly feel lied to and cheated, the same goes for home sales. When a prospective buyer shows up expecting one thing, such as what was shown in the fully-furnished staged photos, only to show up and find the house empty and cold, their excitement level instantly drops. It is better to underpromise and overdeliver so they leave feeling more excited than they previously did.

Get Real!

Your pictures may draw them in, but descriptions are key to ensuring the average viewer understands exactly what they are looking at. The clearer you can be in describing the features and benefits of the home and surrounding neighborhood, the better the odds of weeding out the people who would not find what they are looking for in your house. This ensures only the most qualified and motivated buyers are traipsing through your house on a Sunday afternoon and reduces the time you waste talking with people who get more joy out of touring homes they have no intention of buying than they do making an offer.

Depending on whether you are a licensed agent or a private seller, local laws will vary on what you can or cannot put in writing to avoid potential discrimination or fair housing law violations – and many of them would blow your mind:

- Using a phrase like "within walking distance" can be considered discriminatory to someone who cannot walk.
- "Great schools" would be considered a form of steering.
- "Great for families" would exclude singles.

Yep, it's that crazy. If you are working with a real estate agent, they should know how to word the listing in such a way as to avoid these problems, but it is still helpful to be aware of this. If you are proceeding as an FSBO, then you don't have as much to worry about in terms of legality, but you do still want to craft the most accurate and attractive description of your property beyond just the physical specifications and ensure you are adhering to the discrimination guidelines set forth in the Fair Housing Act. Help potential buyers envision their life in the house by showcasing memories of large holiday gatherings by the fireplace, setting the scene for backyard barbeques in the summer, and anything else a potential buyer can relate to and picture themself doing.

Last, but certainly not least, is the open house. During the pandemic, open houses all but ceased to exist with agents and homeowners finding creative ways to run showings without physically letting people inside. While virtual tours and video walkthroughs experienced some level of success at the time, they were also the only option. With the world open again, there is something to be said for wanting to walk through, breathe in, touch, and smell the home that is about to set you back a few hundred thousand dollars. But a poorly run open house is likely to cause more harm than good as well.

To run an effective open house, you will need people. If you think you can just open the door and let visitors show themselves around, you are sorely mistaken. You don't know any of these people, so why would you want them walking around your home unsupervised? If you plan on escorting them, what do you do when multiple people show up at the same time? It can quickly become a logistical nightmare, and leaving people waiting outside or rushing someone out so the next people can come in will not leave the best impression when they get back home after a long day of house touring.

Beyond just having an adequate number of people on hand to help show the property, some other best practices would be:
- Conduct during daylight hours.
- Have all blinds, drapes, or curtains open to allow natural light in.
- Have all interior doors open.
- Keep all lights on.
- Hide all personal belongings.
- Turn down pictures to protect the identity of loved ones.
- Have water on hand to offer but do not advertise refreshments in your listing.
- Keep a sign-in sheet at the door and make sure guests fill it out completely with their contact information so you can follow up with them a few days later and ask for feedback.

There is a reason the top marketing companies in the world get paid a pretty penny for their work. They understand the science behind what motivates people to make buying decisions for particular products and services, then target them effectively in ways that are tailored specifically to them. Selling real estate is no different. Even some of the best realtors can struggle with marketing strategies in certain markets and wind up employing a trial-and-error methodology.

So, if you are not getting the results you had hoped for, tweak an element of your strategy and reassess. Just don't try changing everything all at once, or you will likely lose sight of what was helpful and what was not.

Buying & Selling Simultaneously

Trying to sell the home you are living in and buying a new one at the same time is one of the most complicated transactions in residential real estate. Knowing now just how many moving parts are involved in a real estate transaction shows why it can already be a stressful process, but multiply that by two and throw time constraints into the mix and it will give you the longest 60 days of your life. Think of it like trying to catch a connecting flight at the airport with only a half-hour window between your first flight landing and the next flight departing. Everything must go exactly according to schedule; otherwise, everything else falls apart.

Logistically speaking, the hardest part about managing this process is that the sellers of the home you are looking to purchase will be wary, or at least they should be, of your situation. There are so many things that can go wrong with the sale of your current home, and each of those has the potential to stall the purchase of the new home. Unless you are fortunate enough to be in a position where you can complete the purchase without first completing the sale, either because you are paying cash or still qualify for a new mortgage while carrying the old one, this is an uphill battle for many reasons.

Potential sellers and their attorneys hate seeing the "contingent on sale" clause in any sales contract. The first and most obvious reason is because there are no guarantees the existing home will ever sell, or sell for what it needs to in order to complete the new transaction. Having the existing home already under contract is a step in the right direction to put the seller's mind at ease, but they must still contend with the reality of that deal falling apart for any of the reasons we mentioned earlier. Lastly is the possibility of you changing your mind about selling or moving in the first place, and then using the contingency to get out of the contract without a penalty.

None of this is to say people do not simultaneously sell and buy homes all the time, because they do. Speak to anyone who has gone through the process and they will likely echo just how stressful it can be. One of the best ways to mitigate some of the stress is to use the same real estate agent for both the sale of one home and the purchase of the other, when physically possible. In situations where the seller is moving far away or out of the market where their current agent is knowledgeable, the next best option is introducing the selling agent to the buying agent so they can coordinate information without having to play telephone through their client.

Team Dynamics

Just because you are on the selling side of the transaction does not mean the need for strong teamwork and communication has changed. Getting the highest price for the sale is often one of the top concerns in this transaction, but a close second is the speed of the transaction. When someone makes the decision to sell their home, they are likely moving on to the next phase of their life, which can be anything from upsizing in the same area, relocating across the country, or moving into an assisted living facility. The longer it takes to get the transaction closed, the more money the seller must spend on payments that are due every month such as the mortgage, taxes, insurance, and utilities.

There are fewer people to communicate with on the selling side of the transaction though, which can simplify the process. Anyone representing a seller does not need to worry about communicating with the inspector, mortgage broker, title company, insurance agent, or appraiser (unless something went drastically wrong in the home valuation, and someone needs to step in and provide data to refute the report). The seller's agent should be in regular communication with the buyer's agent and the seller's attorney (when applicable) to ensure all milestones are being met in a timely fashion so there are no unexpected delays. Making sure the appraisal has been conducted, the report has been submitted to the bank and is satisfactory, and a mortgage commitment has been issued are paramount. If working with a realtor, they will be responsible for confirming this information with the buyer's realtor or the bank, but if you represent yourself, then this will become your responsibility.

For anyone who has not sold a house before, especially without the help of a realtor, it can be difficult getting used to the fact that you cannot just pick up the phone and call whoever you want when questions need to be answered or the process is not going as smoothly as you would like. The buyer's attorney does not work for you and generally will not speak directly with a seller, which means all communication will go through your attorney. If the buyer was working with their own real estate agent, you need to understand their agent only has their buyer's best interests in mind. If the buyers do not have an agent, then you are free to speak directly with them but proceed with caution. It can be very easy to either get too friendly or too pushy, thus opening the door for them to seek more concessions or get turned off completely.

"Real estate cannot be lost or stolen nor can it be carried away. Purchased with common sense, paid for in full, and managed with reasonable care it is about the safest investment in the world."

— Franklin D Roosevelt

Chapter 6: Cash Flow Investing

Cash flow investing is one of the popular real estate strategies many so-called "experts" are trying to push on social media. They focus heavily on the stability and peace of mind that comes with guaranteed income every month, but most leave out the gritty and often arduous task of managing rental properties. Whether you own one unit or one thousand, this is not a hands-off business by any means. It's actually funny people refer to rental income as "passive income" because there is nothing passive about it. Even if you choose to pay a management company to handle the day-to-day operations (which we will discuss in depth in this chapter), your attention will still be required more than you might have previously thought.

None of that is to say owning rental property is a bad idea – just that it is important to set objective expectations. Most of the wealthiest families in the world have built massive real estate empires, and residential rental properties make up a large portion of those holdings. Land is a finite resource, and people always need a roof over their heads, which means you should never struggle to remain at full occupancy – as long as you adhere to the best practices I have found to be successful in scaling a rental business. When done right, owning a substantial real estate portfolio can supplement or replace a full-time income and become a primary source of retirement income.

Believe it or not, the cash flow aspect of owning rental property is not even the best part. In addition to monthly income and real estate being one of the safest investments to own, it has and will continue to appreciate in value over time. This is important because it provides for more options than just being a landlord for the rest of your life. If you decide to sell everything and move to an island when you hit your golden years, chances are, the portfolio will be worth substantially more than you paid for it. You will have a giant nest egg to do with what you please, without having to endure the daily grind of managing your tenants.

Before moving into the mechanics of cash flow investing, remember we will only be looking at residential real estate. There is money to be made in commercial and industrial real estate, as well as land leases and other more exotic options, but they generally require much more specialized knowledge and larger capital investments. During the pandemic, more retail stores went out of business than at any other time since The Great Depression, and the government did not step in to help bail them out of their leases as they did with residential tenants. At the end of the day, people are always going to need a place to live, and renting is much more common than homeownership.

Getting Started

The most important piece in the cash flow investing puzzle comes long before you even start looking for potential deals. Before you do anything, you need to know how you are going to structure your business and protect yourself from liability. Because we live in such a litigious society and some people view all landlords as rich, evil overlords, you cannot take too many precautions in ensuring your assets are protected. This is not intended to provide legal advice, one should always consult with a qualified legal professional when determining what the best options for their business are, which is why lawyers should be part of your dream team. This will only be a guide to the best practices my partners and I use in our own businesses. That being said, the very first thing you need to do is set up a business entity for your rental company.

Setting up your business is a four-step process:
1. Decide the legal structure.
2. File incorporation/organization paperwork with the state.
3. Obtain an Employer Identification Number (EIN) from the IRS.

4. Open a dedicated checking account for the business.

One of the most popular legal structures for real estate investors is a Limited Liability Company (LLC). An LLC can consist of one owner or multiple – there is no limit. Each of these owners will be referred to as "members," unlike in a corporation where the term is "shareholders." When choosing this structure, you have the option of also choosing how it will be treated for taxation purposes. If you are the only member of the LLC, you might opt for the Sole Proprietor option. If you have one or two partners, the Partnership option might be a better choice. But, this is definitely an area where it is best to consult with your CPA prior to making a decision. If you don't already have a great CPA, make sure you get one ASAP.

The S-Corporation is an almost identical structure in terms of legal protections and taxation that can be used in states where LLCs are more difficult to establish. In New York, for example, LLCs are required to "publish" their formation in a certain number of periodicals or journals. There is a cost associated with this that runs upwards of $1K, whereas the cost to establish a corporation is less than $200. In a state like Pennsylvania, there is no publishing requirement for an LLC, so the filing fee is identical to that of a corporation. In states where an LLC might be cost-prohibitive, setting up a corporation can be the better option, although there is one additional hoop to jump through because the "subchapter S" tax status is not something you can do at formation. The company will need to be registered with the state as a C-Corporation, and then a special tax form needs to be completed and sent to the IRS for approval of the S-status. In all the businesses I have started in NY, I have never had the request declined, but in some instances, it has taken months to get the paperwork back. So, make it a point to file long before you have any taxable income, or you will get stuck paying the higher C-Corporation taxes.

No matter which structure you decide to go with, there are options for filing the paperwork. The first is to use a lawyer or legal document preparation service that will file everything on your behalf. If this is your first time setting up a business, it might make sense to pay the extra money for their services and make sure everything is done correctly. If you have done this once or twice, most states have the option of filing yourself on the state website (usually under the Department of State or Secretary of State). The fees are minimal, and you can oftentimes receive a copy of your filing receipt on the spot. This is important because you cannot go any further with banks or lenders without having this paperwork. We have set up nearly two dozen businesses in both PA and NY, and all but the original LLC were done online. It is so easy almost anyone can do it, and the process takes less than ten minutes.

One last thing to say on the legal formation is that the first company you establish should be viewed as the "parent" company. This is the company that will file taxes, receive all rental income, and pay out the expenses. Some investors think what I am about to say is too much work, but in the long run, establishing a separate legal entity for each property you buy will provide the most legal protection. In the event someone sues your company, all assets owned by that company are fair game if the court rules against you. So, if your main entity owns five properties and loses a lawsuit, you could find yourself in a situation where all five houses need to be sold to cover the damages. But, if each property is owned by its own LLC, only one house can be put at risk.

Knowing we just said each entity can be set up in under ten minutes, there is no reason not to take the added protection, and you don't have to go crazy with creative names for each of the additional entities either. In fact, lenders and title companies prefer when you make it easy for them to recognize there is common ownership when deals come across their desks. Since we do several deals a year in the same geographic market, it is beneficial for our partners to know it is us just by glancing at the new LLC name. It could look as simple as this:

Parent company: LAVISH RENTAL PROPERTIES, LLC
Property 1 company: LAVISH 123 MAIN ST, LLC
Property 2 company: LAVISH 234 BROADWAY LLC

Get Real!

In case you didn't catch on, each entity is just getting named by the property address with the first word of the parent company name preceding it. Putting the parent company at the front of each property is what provides name recognition to your partners. Choosing to use the property address in the entity name helps to keep you more organized and avoid having to figure out which entity owns which property. Sure, it may sound more appealing to have catchy names for each entity, but when you own 20 properties, will you really remember that Dynamic Duplex LLC owns the property at 123 Main St? I know I wouldn't!

After you have the main entity filing squared away for your parent company, it is time to apply for your EIN. This is another part of the process where a lawyer or document preparation service can do it for you, but it is so quick and simple that it makes filing the state paperwork to claim your entity name look difficult. A key public service announcement here is to fight the urge to get the EIN number before finishing the state paperwork. The reason is that the company name you want to use might already exist in the state database, which means you will not be able to use it. Once you change the company name, the EIN will no longer be valid, effectively making it a complete waste of time. If you choose to do it yourself, just head over to www.irs.gov and search for the keyword EIN to be redirected to the online application. The entire process takes less than five minutes, and you will be able to download and print the EIN letter on the spot.

Once you have the state filing receipt and EIN letter, it is time to open a business checking account. While it might seem logical to open an account at the same bank where you do your personal banking – and in many cases, it is – don't just take the easy way out. There are several factors that should be taken into consideration, and as a recovering banker, I can confidently say personal convenience is only a small piece of the puzzle. Sure, it's nice to have everything under one roof, but chances are, your business is going to have very different needs from your personal situation, so we will look at a few key areas to take under consideration before settling.

One of the factors we have found to be the most important in a banking relationship is the proximity of branch locations to where you own the properties. No matter how many ways you accept rent payments, there will always be tenants who are late or have an excuse for why they couldn't pay: ran out of checks, don't have online banking; waiting for you to come pick up cash, and the list goes on and on. When you have a bank nearby, you can provide the tenants the business bank account number and have them make their own rent deposits into your account – just make sure to have them write their names on the deposit ticket so it is easier to reconcile your bank statement. We have so many tenants who take advantage of this option that it is the main reason I live over 100 miles away from the closest branch where our business bank is, but all of their branches are within five miles of each property. When you make it easy for people to pay you, money comes in quicker.

Fees and deposit limits are the next key component to evaluating a bank relationship. Unfortunately, banks are not really in the business of providing great customer service as much as they are nickel-and-diming their clients with monthly maintenance fees and a slew of other hidden fees one would never know about unless they took the time to read through all the account disclosures – which no one ever does. Considering this is a business and you are just starting out, a $15-$25 monthly service charge for not meeting a certain minimum balance requirement might be a necessary evil. What you don't want to get stuck with though are limits on how much cash can be deposited in any given month, limits on the number of transactions you can perform, or any other hidden fee that can stunt the growth of your business.

Another feature I find to be incredibly helpful in choosing the best bank is their online and self-service capabilities. We are all busy, and as your business grows, the last thing you are going to want to do is spend hours a week in the bank performing tasks that another bank might have allowed you to perform online. One of the most notable features I can think of is access to Zelle (the service that allows you to transfer money to other people without a charge), especially when you have different banks for both business and personal. It saves the time of having to write yourself checks and wait for them to clear when you want to withdraw money from your business account.

While in the early days you might not yet be ready to buy something, the assortment of lending programs available can also be a deciding factor in which bank to choose. It's a little-known secret that banks value deposit relationships, and the more money you keep in checking and savings accounts with them, the more likely they are to lend you money. In fact, almost every bank my partners and I have ever borrowed money from has always either required a deposit relationship or strongly advised our company to open one to receive the best terms on the lending. This strategy won't take you very far with the larger national banks, as we will learn in the financing chapter, but the smaller regional banks have much more flexibility in their lending guidelines and will often reciprocate.

In a self-service world, many of us would rather just do our own research online and make a decision, but this is one of the few times it would be prudent to hold off on making a final decision until you meet with a banker from the top one or two banks you are considering. Explain to them in detail what the nature of your business is, the expected activity, and plans for the future. They will be able to point out all the ways they can accommodate those needs and clearly outline any extra fees you might be subjected to. It is also helpful to have a familiar name and face in the event there is ever an issue you need assistance with.

At the end of the day, you may never find one bank that has every feature and service you would like, but that's okay. As your business grows, you may need to work with multiple banks or switch entirely. Also, don't rule out being creative when need be. I cannot live without Zelle or online account transfers between banks, but none of my local banks that provide us with financing offer either as an option. I can't even move money between two of them without walking into one for a withdrawal and then crossing the street to make a deposit. However, my personal bank does offer external account transfers and Zelle, so I made the decision to add each business bank account as an external transfer option on my personal accounts. Now, when money needs to be moved, I can pull it from one bank into my personal account and then push it to the other bank where I need the funds.

The last thing you need to get your business off the ground is a good deal or two. This isn't always as easy as successful investors may make it seem depending on where you live, your budget, and how strong the real estate market is at the time. Despite all those factors, good deals can be found anywhere at any time if you are patient and disciplined in doing the work. For a comprehensive list of ways to identify potential deals, refer back to the chapter on deal finding, then proceed to the next section on how to evaluate those deals.

Evaluating Deals

In the process of deal finding, you likely looked at hundreds of properties, most of which never became viable options for one reason or another. I can look at a property listing and usually know within a few seconds if it deserves more attention. Based on the specific criteria you are looking for, a number of factors, like price, location, or type, could easily disqualify a property from consideration, but when something does catch your eye, and holds your attention for slightly longer than others, it's time to evaluate whether or not it is worth pursuing.

Cash flow investing is slightly different from flipping and wholesaling, which we will discuss in Chapters 7 and 8, in regard to property value. With most other strategies, acquiring the property at the lowest possible price is the most important factor in determining whether or not it has the potential to be profitable. That's not to say you should want to overpay for a cash flow property, just that it is not nearly as important since you will likely hold it for a few years, during which time there will be appreciation. What really matters with a rental property is the potential net income, which can be calculated fairly simply by using a basic subtraction formula. A fillable tool is available on our website at www.timeawaygroup.com for your convenience as well.

Gross Rent
- Mortgage Payment
- Property Taxes
- Insurance
- Utilities*
- Management Fees
- Vacancy Rate (Gross Rent X 5%-10%, depending on how conservative you want to be)
- Misc. Expenses (5%-10%)

NET INCOME

*Never take the amount a seller or listing agent represents as the true utility number. Not every seller is trying to actively deceive you, but the truth is, most are not really sure what their actual utility numbers are. If the accounts are on autopay and they own several properties, it is likely all they see every month is a series of debits from the electric, gas, and water companies. They might still be using the estimated utilities the owner before them provided when they took ownership. The best way to ensure you do not get stuck in a situation where the utilities are far more than expected is to request the 12-month statements for every utility the owner pays. In addition, confirm with the seller if the property was at full occupancy for the entire year. Vacant apartments are not likely to use much heat, electricity, or water, so the statements will be irrelevant if there were substantial vacancies.

The net income number itself is important because it represents the amount of money you stand to take home every month in profit. There is no right or wrong number as it will depend on how much you paid for the property, how much of your own money you put as a down payment, and how conservative your estimates are. There are a few other ratios that can help shed some more light on how profitable an investment really is once you arrive at the net income number, which is the basis for all calculations.

Before we can dive deeper into profitability ratios, we need to really focus on the gross rent number since it is the basis for everything and can be the most ambiguous depending on how familiar you are with the local market. Fair Market Rent (FMR) refers to what an average apartment of a certain size is likely to rent for in a specific area. This number is not set by anyone and is completely driven by the market. The FMR for a one-bedroom apartment in parts of Manhattan might be upwards of $4,000, while a similar unit in upstate NY may only have an FMR of $1,200.

There are a few ways to get an idea of what the FMR could be in your target market. The first, and most accurate for at least one type of tenant, is by using what the Department of Housing and Urban Development (HUD) considers to be the maximum rent they will pay on behalf of housing-subsidized tenants, more commonly referred to as Section 8 tenants. These guidelines and rent limits are readily available on their website and can vary from one zip code to the next, so it is important to make sure you are not generalizing. In some markets, HUD may pay less than what would be considered FMR for a private-pay tenant, but in other areas, they will actually pay more.

To get an idea of what the private-pay market will bear for rents, there are three main evaluation techniques, and we will rank them in order from least accurate to most reliable. The first is to look online at what apartments are currently being listed at. If you're noticing a trend of all one-bedroom apartments listed within a certain price range, it could be considered a decent benchmark. The only issue here is you have no way of knowing if any of those units actually rented for that price. The second method would be to join local landlord and property management groups and see what other landlords in your market are currently collecting for their units. The last and the absolute best way to assess rent is by working with a local realtor who can search the Multiple Listing Service (MLS) for historical data on what apartments have actually been rented for.

Working with a real estate professional for your renting needs can alleviate much of the stress that goes into finding and screening tenants, arranging showings, and weeding through offers. A real estate agent will take photographs of your unit, help you determine the best rent to charge, arrange all showings so you do not need to be there, collect financial documentation and credit scores, and only present you with offers from the most qualified tenants. Real estate agents are compensated for this service, and it is generally calculated as an amount equal to one month's rent, or in high-priced areas like Manhattan as much as 15% of the annual rent amount. Depending on the market you operate in, this commission might get paid by the landlord or it could be paid by the tenant. Because of this, many landlords will be pennywise and pound-foolish in avoiding a realtor to save the commission, but in the long run, it can wind up being the best money you ever spent. Good tenants are priceless, and bad tenants can quickly turn a positive cash flow negative.

Now it's time to discuss what really matters – profitability. This is where only looking at the net income number can be misleading. While net income will show how much actual profit should make it to your bank account every month, it falls short of truly comparing how one deal may stack up against another. But how can that be if profit is king, right? While that cannot be argued completely, it can be put in perspective to realize how sometimes a property with a net income of $500 per month could still be a better option than one bringing in $1K per month after combining a few other factors.

The capitalization rate, or "cap rate," as it is commonly referred to, is by far one of the most important metrics to use in any type of deal where you might be using some of your own cash and/or involving a bank. If the seller is financing the entire purchase, which we learned about in Chapter 2, then I would not be so concerned with the cap rate because any net income is pure profit without tying up any capital or resources. There are many places where you can find definitions of the term cap rate, but for the purposes of this book, we will simply define it as the net income divided by the value of the property in question. Here is what that would look like for a property worth $500K that has a monthly net income of $2K:

$2,000 x 12 = $24,000 / $500,000 = 4.8%

125

In the above scenario, your effective cap rate is 4.8%. Does that sound like a good return? Once again, the answer is subjective and needs to be compared accordingly. The answer will vary depending on whether you are comparing the return to all other available investment options or strictly to real estate. At face value, against stock market investment options like the S&P 500, where average returns have been over 10%, it might not seem as attractive. However, that does not take into consideration the potential for the appreciation in value of the property over time in addition to the rental income, so it would be best not to try comparing real estate returns in this manner. The better option is to consider the return based on the geographic market.

In the NYC metro real estate market at the time of writing this book, 4.8% would not be considered a bad cap rate. Property values are among the highest in the nation, and many rents are government-regulated for fair housing purposes. However, in the more rural markets we invest in, I will not accept any cap rate under 9%, with 12%-15% being my usual target. I might make far less net income on a 12% cap rate in PA than I would with the 4.8% in NYC, but my leverage is much higher, allowing me to buy multiple properties for the same investment someone would need to make to acquire one in the city.

The other metric that is incredibly useful for evaluating real estate returns when you are using any amount of your own cash would be the "cash-on-cash" return, or the percentage gain made on any net income in comparison to the amount of cash you invested in the deal, whether it be for a down payment or an all-cash transaction. Because cash is king, this is a metric we want to pay extra attention to. To demonstrate the calculation, we will use the same scenario as we did for the cap rate, where the property was worth $500K with a monthly net income of $2K, only this time we are going to assume two different scenarios so you can truly see the difference leverage makes.

Scenario #1: The only cash used in this transaction was a standard 25% down payment.

$2,000 x 12 = $24,000 / $125,000 (25% down payment) = 19.2%

Scenario #2: The entire deal was paid in cash.

$2,000 x 12 = $24,000 / $500,000 (100% paid in cash) = 4.8%

I swear, it is just a coincidence that the cash-on-cash return in Scenario 2 is the same as the cap rate. The important thing to note here is you made four times more return by putting down 75% less cash. If I had $500K lying around and needed to decide how to approach this deal, it would be a no-brainer for me to go with the 25% down payment option while saving the other $375K for down payments on three other properties of the same value, or investing it in the stock market's S&P 500 to diversify my portfolio while taking advantage of their historical annual return of 10%+ instead of tying it up at 4.8%. But there are exceptions to every rule, and sometimes you cannot just look at the numbers.

Why in the world would I just say that after spending all this time going through the numbers? It's the foundation, so you can have the most basic criteria for evaluating deals as a new investor. As you grow, learn, and negotiate more deals, you will see opportunities these calculations might not take into account. For example, let's assume the $500K property in question is in utter disrepair and no bank will lend on it, leaving you no choice but to pay all cash if you really wanted it. However, the after-renovation value could be one million dollars. Even if you spend another $200K on the renovations, there is now another $300K of profit built in that you might have overlooked if only accounting for the straight calculations.

The key takeaway from this section should not be how to secure only the most profitable deals, although that is of paramount importance for longevity. The bigger lesson is that every investor is different and every deal is different. What might be a good deal for one investor in a particular market might not be such a great deal for the same investor in another market or a second investor in the same market. Heck, based on changing market conditions, what might have been considered a good deal for me last year might not be viewed quite as highly this year. You need to be happy and comfortable with the projections before moving forward. If a deal seems like too much work for the amount of profit, walk away regardless of what the calculations say. Remember, real estate is not *passive*, and your time can quickly become the one variable that is hard to put a value on!

Tenants

Tenants are the biggest variable and double-edged sword in cash flow investing. You can't be in the residential real estate rental business without tenants, yet tenants can quickly become the bane of your existence. Countless landlords sell properties every year because of issues with their tenants and the amount of time and money it drains from them. Not all tenant issues can be predicted or avoided though. Sometimes, things just happen in life that put a previously great tenant into a bad position, and depending on where you are doing business, the laws on how you can deal with these problem tenants vary greatly.

In the NYC metropolitan area, it often feels like your tenants have more rights to your property than you do. The eviction process can easily drag on for six months or more, judges are notorious for always taking the tenant's side in any dispute, and most tenants have learned how to use the system to their personal advantage. In certain other markets, you can get an eviction within six weeks if you show reasonable cause and pay the corresponding court fees. There are some really landlord-friendly markets where an eviction can happen within three weeks, and the local marshal will come to put their belongings on the curb. Never underestimate just how important the legal landscape can be for landlords.

Now that we know what our net income, cap rate, and cash-on-cash return are and what they mean for your profitability, let's look at what this could mean using extreme examples on both sides that will take into account the soft costs of owning real estate when income is not being generated. Both scenarios will have equal elements, meaning each building will have the same number of units at the same monthly rent and expenses for the same net income:

$1,100 net income
Apt 1: $1,100
Apt 2: $1,200
Apt 3: $1,000

When all tenants are paying their rent, the net income for the year should be $13,200 ($1,100 x 12). Each will also have a tenant who has stopped paying rent. The only difference will be landlord-friendly versus tenant-friendly jurisdictions.

Scenario #1: Landlord-friendly jurisdiction

The tenant in apartment 2 stops paying rent and needs to be evicted, which takes six weeks. We will be generous and assume the landlord was able to get new tenants within two weeks, so the total rent lost was $2,400. This now reduces the annual profit down to $10,800, or $900 per month. Not an ideal situation, but the owner has still made money for the year and can chalk the lost rent up to the cost of doing business.

Scenario #2: Tenant-friendly jurisdiction

The tenant in apartment 2 stops paying rent and needs to be evicted, which takes six months. Because this has dragged on so long, we are going to have to assume, because it is usually the case, that the apartment has been destroyed. In a best-case scenario, it will take a full month to get the repairs done and ready for the next tenants, meaning the total rent lost on the unit is $8,400. This now reduces the annual profit to $4,800, or $400 per month, which is less than half the amount in Scenario 1. That is not a large enough cushion to offset any other unexpected expenses that may arise and can quickly push this landlord into losing money for the year.

If you are going to have a successful career in renting residential real estate, finding good tenants is just as important as finding profitable deals. When it comes to allowing someone to live in an asset you own, there is no such thing as being too thorough in your screening process. I've watched many landlords accept questionable tenants who provided a few choice pieces of information to show they qualified because they were afraid of asking too many questions or scaring the prospective tenant off. The truth of the matter is, good tenants are not going to be turned off by your thorough approach. Anyone who walks away because you asked for a reference, a credit report, or any of the other items we are about to cover was probably going to be more of a headache than they were worth anyway.

The most basic qualification every landlord should ask for, even if they choose to ask for nothing else, is proof of income. The bare minimum proof of income should consist of the two most recent years' tax returns and the most current 60 days' worth of paystubs. It does not matter if they are still working for the same company reflected on the tax returns from two years ago; the key is to show consistent earnings in line with the minimum requirements you expect from a tenant. People change jobs all the time so that in itself is not necessarily a red flag. However, if you notice a trend of multiple different employers from one year to the next, it could be a sign they do not keep jobs very long and shows them to be at risk for unemployment during their tenancy.

An additional layer of protection would be to also ask for an employment verification letter, which is simply a document on company letterhead signed by their immediate supervisor to certify they currently work there, or you can make a follow-up call to reconfirm that information. It might seem excessive, but as you become more experienced in real estate, one of the most painful lessons is about the great lengths people will go to deceive you when it is in their best interest or you have something they want. If you wind up having serious concerns about the validity of the information you are getting, cross reference all documents against a photo identification to make sure they are not pulling a bait-and-switch by applying with someone else's credentials.

Get Real!

There may be certain instances where a prospective tenant is unable or unwilling to provide the standard income verification, and those situations should be handled on a case-by-case basis as judgment and intuition might lead you to make an exception for a candidate who seems like a good fit. For instance, a Section 8 tenant does not have to prove income because their housing voucher is considered proof of their ability to pay. A younger person just starting out in life, who just got their first job, will not have the work experience to provide everything you asked for, but if they can prove they recently landed a six-figure job with a major company like Apple, it might be worth taking a chance on them. To that same point, you could also ask for a cosigner who will share in the responsibility of making rent payments.

Before we jump into income requirements, I want to mention Section 8 tenants. There is a stigma associated with Section 8 tenants that has led many landlords to choose not to rent to them. Besides just being a violation of the Fair Housing Act depending on how many units the landlord owns, the overall belief that these tenants are high risk, low quality, or some type of nuisance is no more true than what could be said for a random private-pay tenant you don't know at all. In our own business, we have experienced more issues with private-pay tenants than we ever have with Section 8 tenants. As long as you understand the process and requirements, Section 8 rents are always paid on time, and the tenants are generally there for longer than the average private-pay tenant, which significantly decreases your vacancy rates and makes the business more profitable. When possible, make connections with the people who work at the local Section 8 office and let them know you are a landlord. Our experience has shown they always have a waiting list of tenants looking for apartments, which will allow you to fill any vacancies quicker than through other means.

If you don't want to work with Section 8 tenants, you will have to find and screen all your potential tenants. We always start with income because it is the most clear-cut, easy-to-understand, and applicable metric one can use to determine a tenant's ability to pay. But income is only a factor in deciding if they *can* pay, not if they are *likely* to pay. Someone can make exponentially more than is required but be irresponsible or derelict in making those payments. That is why we leverage a recent credit score and report to determine how responsible someone has been in the past. The reason for the credit score and report is simply because the score itself might not give much insight into someone's track record.

Credit scores range depending on which bureau one uses, and as a society, we have become trained to believe that any scores under 750 or 700 make a person unworthy of credit or trust with our rentals. Sadly, nothing could be further from the truth. Twenty-plus years ago, I had a credit score of 815, but that score was based entirely on my limited credit history (which was positive) and could not predict my first venture into real estate would result in multiple foreclosures. Today, my credit score is a lousy 620, yet there is not a single blemish on my report. Because credit inquiries and usage limits largely determine the score, I now appear like a risk because I have multiple banks pulling my credit every quarter, and there are millions of dollars in outstanding mortgages.

When you dig deeper into the facts it becomes clear I was a much bigger risk as a college graduate with an *excellent* credit score than I am today in my forties with a *poor* credit score. The same can happen with your tenants. If the income supports the rental and I feel the tenant would be a good fit, then I will dive deeper into their credit report to see if any major red flags jump out at me. Normally, these red flags would consist of:

- Payments 30+ days late
  - Reported as either 30+, 60+, or 90+, the longer they are late, the worse it reflects.
- Charged-off accounts
  - Delinquent accounts the original creditor has closed but not taken any other action against them for recovery.
- Active collection accounts
  - Delinquent accounts the original creditor has sold to a collection agency.
- Foreclosure

- o Having any real estate repossessed by the bank.
- Bankruptcy
  - o The legal process through which people or other entities who cannot repay debts to creditors may seek relief from some or all of their debts. In most jurisdictions, bankruptcy is imposed by a court order, often initiated by the debtor.

Considering we are still in the territory of art meeting science to make the best possible decision on which tenants to rent to and who to avoid, there is one more creative way of getting additional peace of mind. Asking for a prior landlord reference is a great way of determining why the tenant is leaving their last apartment and what the landlord thought about them. Suffice it to say, no tenant in their right mind is going to provide a reference if they are leaving on bad terms, so caution is still needed. Some will make up a story for why they don't have a reference, but others will make up a reference by putting down the contact information for a friend or relative. To avoid falling for this trap, take extra steps to ensure the person listed as the reference was actually the landlord by doing some leg work:

- Use Truepeoplesearch.com to see if their name and phone number match the prior address.
- Ask the landlord to verify the dates they lived there to see if it matches what the tenant says.
- Ask the tenant to show you canceled checks or other proof of rent payments to the person they claim was their landlord.
- Ask the current landlord to sign a letter (estoppel) certifying the tenant was paid and current.

At the end of the day, these steps are just ways to mitigate risk. The more you implement, the lower your risk exposure, but nothing is foolproof. If someone wants to be deceitful, they can usually find a way. Heck, there are some landlords out there who will give the worst tenants in the world a glowing recommendation just to get them to move out and become someone else's problem. So, when in doubt, listen to your gut. If your intuition supports the belief that the tenant feels like a problem, listen to it. There will always be plenty of other people in need of housing. It is better to forego one or two months of rent in search of a perfect tenant than to rent immediately only to get stuck with a headache.

Leases

Leases, much like any other type of contract or agreement, are nothing more than words on paper if you do not know exactly what is stated and have the legal means to fall back on that wording should you ever find yourself in a court proceeding for any landlord/tenant dispute. A lease should not be treated as a formality just so you can collect the rent and security deposit and move on. The purpose of a lease goes far beyond just letting a tenant know how much their rent is. It is to set clear expectations for everything you can imagine from the time the tenant moves in and for the entire term of the lease. Most landlord/tenant disputes would never happen if the wording was clear and transparent, and the landlord took the time to review each section with the tenant instead of assuming they read and understood it. Almost no one reads it, and most skip straight to the signature page after making sure the rental amount is accurate.

There is no right or wrong way to structure a lease or present it in writing. Some landlords prefer to use standard forms available through a local Board of Realtors, some will have their attorney draft all leases, and others will type something up themselves based on what a friend or relative advised. I have seen leases as short as two pages and as long as 27. The length and logical order of the contents do not matter nearly as much as the content you choose to include.

One of the most critical places to start is with the security deposit and the condition of the apartment prior to moving a new tenant in. The return of security deposits at the end of a lease can become one of the most contentious issues of the tenancy. Tenants are notorious for not leaving units in the condition they were rented in or for breaking the lease early and still expecting their money to be returned. While there is little that can be done to mitigate the second issue short of having very clear wording on how much notice needs to be given prior to terminating a lease, the condition of the unit can easily be documented before a tenant ever moves in. Take the time to walk through the unit with them, taking pictures of everything and notating anything that needs to be fixed before them moving in, as well as anything they are going to live with but don't want to be held responsible for later. These photos and notes can be stored on your computer, uploaded to a file-sharing service like Google Drive and Dropbox, or printed out for filing in a physical folder.

Tying in with security deposits is the subject of pets. In certain markets, it is almost impossible to even find a rental unit where pets are allowed. The higher the demand for rentals and the more expensive the living cost, the less likely a landlord is going to be to accept pets and the inherent risk of damage that comes with them. Then, there are other markets where it is just expected pets will be allowed, and the only question is how many and what type. For those who do choose to accept pets, it often comes with the trade-off of an increased security deposit. Whether you are an animal lover or not, the truth of the matter is not all pet owners are responsible or attentive, and any animal not properly cared for can quickly become a liability the landlord will need to pay for before renting the unit back out to a new tenant.

Pets can be a very sensitive topic for many, and local laws vary on what a landlord can or cannot restrict. For instance, if they choose to allow dogs, many municipalities will not allow for discrimination against sizes or breeds. Pet rent, which is basically an additional security deposit, is acceptable in some places and not others. The only hard and fast rule is that service animals are not considered pets under federal law, meaning even landlords who do not want pets have no choice but to accept the service animal. For all other pet questions, familiarize yourself with state and local laws.

Utilities are the next section in the lease to pay particular attention to. A landlord's best friends are units that come with separate gas and electric meters. Including utilities in the rental amount should be avoided at all costs when you have the ability to make the tenant pay for them. If it is a single-family home, the tenant should also be made responsible for the water bill. Although this is the one utility it is impossible to make the tenants pay for in any type of multifamily property scenario, as almost no homes have multiple water meters.

Beyond just saving you money every month, having tenants pay for their own utilities also ensures they are more responsible with regard to their usage. When they do not have to worry about the electric bill, tenants are more likely to pump the air conditioning on full blast with windows open in the summer, or crank the heat up in the winter and crack a window when it gets too hot instead of lowering the temperature in the winter. If you are in a position where it is not possible to separate the utilities, be sure to have wording in your lease that makes the tenant liable for any bills excessively over the average consumption so they have some motivation to be responsible.

Subletting is another often overlooked section of the lease that should be given an honorable mention here. This has become a very popular practice with the rise of short-term vacation rentals such as Airbnb, where someone will represent themselves as a tenant but then turn around and rent the unit or individual rooms out on a shorter-term basis so they can make a profit. In a capitalist world, there might not seem to be anything wrong with this situation so long as the lessee is able to pay the landlord the rent as agreed upon every month, but it does open the door to potential legal issues should a sub-lessee cause damage or refuse to leave. If your lease did not expressly prohibit this practice, you might find yourself going to court with the sub-lessee and not your original tenant.

While you, as the property owner, more than likely have homeowner's insurance to protect your investment, that is not always enough to protect your tenants and their belongings. After many years of not requiring our tenants to maintain a renter's insurance policy or at least stipulating in the lease that we advise they maintain one and that we would not be held liable for any damage or theft, we have now made it a standard practice. It only takes one flood or other catastrophic event to create ambiguity and financial strain. If a tenant is not required to have their own insurance and suffers a loss, they will likely come after you for damages. If a unit becomes uninhabitable and the tenants need to be temporarily relocated, your homeowner's policy will not cover the cost of a hotel, but their renter's insurance will.

On the topic of catastrophic events, maintenance issues are another area of the lease where it pays to be extremely specific. As a landlord, you are responsible for most things that break inside and outside a tenant's unit, but not everything. Certain items, like clogged toilets, replacing light bulbs, or painting walls should be clearly marked as the responsibility of the tenant. Can you imagine what would happen if you had 50 tenants all calling you every month to change their light bulbs and plunge their toilets? But you also don't want to deter people from notifying you about minor issues that can become bigger problems like leaky faucets or leaks in the roof.

Another particularly important section of the lease has to do with a "notice to quit," which is just a legal way of referring to the notice you must provide someone before filing eviction proceedings against them. This varies from one local jurisdiction to the next, and it is best to consult with a housing lawyer before putting this wording into your lease. In places like NYC, having a lease where the tenant has waived their right to a notice to quit will not stand up in court. In other places where our company has done business, it is legal and customary to ask a tenant to waive this right before moving in. Generally, the only people who have a problem with this are the ones who are most likely to default and need that protection anyway.

Saving the best, and arguably most important, for last, always clearly stipulate payment dates, options for remittance, and penalties for delinquency so you can avoid ever needing to enforce a notice to quit. Even if a tenant moved in on a date other than the first of the month, it is better to prorate their first month's rent and still have their lease and rent due date made effective the first of the month. When you only have one or two units it might not be such a big deal to have two different payment dates, but as you acquire more tenants, it will become increasingly difficult to remember whose rent is due on what date. Also, give your tenants as many payment options as possible to increase the percentage of on-time payments. If you currently only accept checks by mail, there are numerous ways the payment can get delayed. If you also offer the option of Zelle, Venmo, or a building management payment portal such as Buildium, then you greatly increase the speed with which funds are received.

Daily Operations

Deciding on whether or not to manage your investment properties or hire a third-party management company can be one of the most crucial questions when building your residential real estate empire. It is also another area where there is no right or wrong answer – everything depends on your personal preference for how hands-on you can and want to be. Plus, there are some additional logistical concerns we will cover in detail. It is natural to want to do everything yourself, and early on, that approach is advisable since it gives you a firsthand understanding of all the work that goes into managing property. This way, if you do decide to bring in a professional management company, you will have a better idea of their scope of work, and it will make it easier to stay on top of them and ensure they are not taking advantage of you with additional fees or extra expenses.

The first and, by far, most important factor to take into consideration before hiring a property manager is your personal ability level and time constraints. To effectively manage rental properties on your own, one must have a basic understanding of all things mechanical. If not, it will be easy to panic and make giant issues out of things that are not such a big deal or to minimize the impact of other items and allow them to become bigger problems down the road. The second part of that equation is also whether you have the time and bandwidth to handle issues as they arise. Working a full-time job, raising a family, and managing rental units all directly conflict with one another, and the best of intentions may leave you spread too thin.

The next criteria would be how many units you own and how they are distributed. Managing a five-unit apartment building will be logistically easier than owning five single-family ones spread out around town. There is no magic number for how many units is too many, and the decision will likely become a combination of factors. Each unit you add to your portfolio is another tenant to communicate with, rent payment to collect, maintenance and upkeep to coordinate, and the potential for phone calls in the middle of the night.

The geographic proximity between where you live and where your rental units are will also be a critical factor in whether or not it makes sense to outsource the management. We could spend an entire chapter about the risks associated with being an absentee landlord or someone who lives two-plus hours away from their rental units. It's not that you will need to stop by on a daily basis, but when a need arises, the prospect of spending four hours roundtrip to address it becomes a bit of a nuisance after the first or second occurrence. There are valid reasons to invest outside of your own geographic area even though you cannot be physically present, but trying to manage any number of units from a distance will prove problematic.

The one factor that should never be an issue when deciding whether or not to hire a management company is money. Each property you buy should generate enough profit to cover all expenses, including a management fee. If it doesn't, you shouldn't buy it – plain and simple. If you are thinking of hiring a management company, let's take a closer look at what they can do for you and what they expect in return. Typically, a property manager will charge a fee equal to somewhere between 7.5%-15% of your gross monthly rent roll. The more units they manage for you, the closer to the 7.5% range you can expect to see, which reinforces why it might not make the most sense to outsource management when you only own one or two units. However, don't just look at the money spent on the service.

When interviewing potential management companies, there are several areas to pay close attention to as they will be the ones that wind up saving or costing you the most time. For full disclosure, we do not pay a management company for any of our properties, but that is because we have the infrastructure in place to not only manage everything in-house but also offer our services to other property owners. Every property is unique and will likely have one-off situations to be dealt with, but the basics of rent collection, tenant relations, and property upkeep will always be present.

By far one of the biggest reasons property owners engage with outside management companies or on-site superintendents is to handle the headaches that come with maintenance issues. Everyone underestimates the amount of work involved in managing rental properties because they have been sold on this notion of "passive income." Things break. Tenants have disagreements with each other. Anything that can possibly go wrong will eventually go wrong. In fact, it is highly likely multiple things will go wrong at the same time. Depending on your threshold for fielding midnight phone calls, scheduling contractors, inspecting repair work, and paying bills, this can get old very quickly.

A management company can take this all off your hands. We always ask the clients we manage property for if they have preferred service people to use in the event something breaks, and we make a note of that in their files. Then, we establish a maximum monthly amount we are approved to use for service issues without getting permission each time. So, if a client gives us a $500 threshold for the month and the repair costs anything less, we will simply dispatch the appropriate provider, confirm the work was completed, pay the contractor, and recoup the money spent from the rents we collect while sending the client a monthly breakdown. If a client has questions at the end of the month, they only need to make one phone call for clarification and can rest assured they did not need to waste hours of their own time throughout the month.

Just about tied for the top concern amongst landlords is rent collection. Money can make people do crazy things, and when it is your money at stake, emotions can run high. Many landlords want to go knock on doors and demand payment, toss around threats, and do other things that only make the situation more volatile. A management company may have a financial interest in rent collection since they do not get paid on amounts they do not collect, but they know the proper steps to handle collections without getting emotionally involved.

Some landlords will also wind up feeling bad for a tenant when they don't pay and make concessions out of the kindness of their heart. You know the "Pay me next week," or "Sure, we can waive the late fees" type of statements to avoid conflicts. All this does is set a precedent for the person to take advantage in the future. Yes, there are good people who wind up in bad situations from time to time, but experience dictates the majority of the time this behavior continues and gets worse. A management company has no personal attachment to any one tenant and will treat everyone equally. It's amazing how quickly a tenant, who does not pay and gives their landlord a sob story, suddenly has all the money needed once a property manager serves them with an eviction notice.

We covered the matter of tenants extensively already, but this is another area the property manager can assist with. Outside of providing them with your rental criteria for income, credit, and pet restrictions, they will go to work marketing, screening, and leasing your units without you ever needing to meet anyone face to face unless you choose to. They will set the expectations for rent payments, collect the money, and file for evictions when needed. Considering they do not get paid on unpaid rent, it is in their best interest to find you the best possible tenants.

Paying and reconciling bills is another pain point that increases as the business grows. It never sounds like a lot upfront, but each property you own could have anywhere from six-plus payments due every month. Between the mortgage, taxes, insurance, electric, gas, water, sewerage, and other ancillary expenses, a two-family home could have you writing out 12 checks each month. Sure, you can have everything set up on autopay so those bills never come across your desk, but then you are missing the opportunity to check the numbers every month to make sure nothing is out of whack. There's nothing worse than realizing three months too late that an electric bill has been triple what it should be because you have no recourse – and sadly, it has happened to us on more than one occasion in the early days.

Last, but certainly not least, is the luxury of having someone who can go to court for you when those nasty eviction proceedings roll around. If time was already a concern, nothing wastes more of it than having to deal with the courts. First, you have to take the steps to show a tenant they are in danger of being evicted, which usually requires posting a notice on their door. Next, you have to physically appear in the courthouse to file for the court date. Then, you have to appear again for the hearing, which at times might require more than one appearance in court. All of this is per eviction and can quickly make it feel like you live in the courthouse. As your legally appointed agent, the management company can appear on your behalf and put all that time back into your day.

Expense Management

Several of the topics in this chapter have already been briefly touched on, but along with rent collection, expense management is one of the biggest determining factors in your company's profitability. When evaluating deals, we left a buffer in the calculations for a 10% increase in expenses just to ensure if there is an off month where usage is high, you will not be left in the negative. But, if you are relatively new to cash flow investing, it is advisable to increase that number to 15% or 20% until you have a better handle on what the true numbers are.

Hopefully, you followed the advice from earlier in this chapter and made sure to obtain 12 months' worth of bills for each utility you will be paying to confirm the monthly average is in line with what the seller told you. That is only the first step though, and it will not keep you from running into potential issues. Anything can go wrong at any given time, and the outward signs are not always visible. Sometimes the only way to find out about a bigger issue is by inspecting your utility bills every month, but if you are still wondering what could possibly cause a profitable investment to turn negative, we will look at some case studies of situations we have found ourselves in over time.

Depending on where you own property, water bills can be one of the most expensive utilities you cannot avoid paying. Larger cities tend to have more affordable water bills, and many very rural areas might have well water, which means no water bill at all. Most places that fall somewhere between a big city and a country farm will have private water companies, such as Suez or AquaAmerica, who are responsible for delivering the water. Aqua happens to be the water provider for all our properties, and the average monthly cost for a two-family home is about $100. Imagine our surprise when we saw a few $700+ charges on our bank statements from Aqua. Upon further investigation, we realized one of our four-family homes was getting charged more than triple what the bill should have been (and no, they will never proactively tell you that your usage is higher than usual).

After asking Aqua to come out and check the water meter, only to find out it was functional, we were left with no choice but to inspect each unit one by one. Only then did we find out two units had toilets that took hours to fill, one unit had several leaks in the kitchen and bathroom, and the fourth unit had four additional people living there. All these discoveries were issues on multiple levels. The slow toilets and leaks could cause structural damage and mold over time, and the extra inhabitants were in violation of the lease. They all also cost us a significant amount of money. Had we not reviewed the bank statements and utility bills, those increased costs could have continued for months.

The same thing can happen when dealing with electric and gas usage, especially where heat is concerned. If you have ever paid one of these bills on your own home or apartment, you probably understand that feeling in the summer when you hesitate to turn on the air conditioning for fear of a massive electric bill or keep the heat at a steady 65 degrees in the winter to avoid the extra costs. Well, your tenants do not have the same concern for your wallet and will almost always place their personal comfort and convenience above yours. For larger buildings with only one meter, it could be hard to figure out who the culprit is, but you can pay attention to patterns. For instance, if your bill has always been fairly consistent yet spiked in the last two months, take a look at what could be different. Do you have a new tenant? Did an existing tenant move more people in without telling you?

Inspections of the units themselves go hand in hand with regular monitoring of expenses. Yes, an inspection can help figure out what is wrong, but that is a hindsight move. You have already overpaid for a month or more before realizing there was a problem, but if you have a regular maintenance and inspection schedule, you will be more likely to catch some of these problems before the money begins adding up. A broken window may cost a hundred dollars to fix, but the money it can save in winter might be exponentially more. The same holds true for leaks in apartments like we already spoke about but can be extended to the mechanical systems themselves. Boilers, water heaters, pumps, and anything else mechanical needs routine service to perform at optimal levels and extend their useful life.

A regular maintenance schedule will also keep you prepared for when larger expenditures might be expected. When a trained professional tells you a mechanical system is nearing the end of its useful life, it is better to start budgeting for a replacement right away instead of waiting for it to malfunction in the most epic and costly way possible – which it always does. Also, make notes of the small improvements you can make here and there when cash flow allows you to become more operationally efficient in the future by helping to reduce utility costs, such as:

- Low flow water fixtures
- Low flow toilets
- LED lighting
- Energy efficient windows
- Attic insulation

Get Real!

When it comes to making repairs or upgrades, get in the habit of looking for bulk sales on items or discontinued items you can stock up on when cash flow allows. We always try to use the same material in all our units so we can buy in bulk and always have what we need on hand. Whether it be flooring, toilets, electrical fixtures, paint, or anything else each of your units will need, not having to scramble for something at the moment is bound to save money in the long run. If you don't have the storage space, get creative and consider using basements or garages in the property you own instead of renting them out for additional income. Your money will go further stockpiling these items than it would ever get you in monthly rent.

The final issue to stay on top of is property taxes. This can be a big one, but because they don't happen routinely, many people never even think about it until after they are already losing money. Property taxes are easy to verify when you first make a purchase. It is also easy enough to make a phone call and find out if a reassessment is on the horizon for the upcoming year. But what happens two or three years down the road when the local municipality raises taxes across the board and you are not aware of it until after the fact? If your tenants are already under active leases, you cannot quickly raise rent to offset it, and you likely will not want to sell in a hurry over something that could have been addressed earlier on. Stay in the know by joining mailing lists for local homeowners associations, business development organizations, and even the municipality's email list so you can start planning changes before you are already in the red.

"A pessimist sees the difficulty in every opportunity; an optimist sees the opportunity in every difficulty."

— Winston Churchill

Chapter 7: Flip Investing

HGTV has more than enough shows geared toward the glamorous lifestyle of a house flipper to convince anyone they are just one remodeling job away from becoming the next *Property Brothers* or *Flip or Flop*. Let's look at that in the context of other areas of life and the fake reality television feeds us. These days, everyone thinks they can be a YouTube star, Instagram influencer, or other kinds of reality stars. If that was possible for the masses, there would no longer be an appeal to it. Although every kid grows up dreaming of becoming a professional athlete at some point, less than a fraction of a percent actually make it to the major leagues. The potential is there, but the struggle is also real. The difference between failing at any of the other ambitions mentioned is only a waste of your time and possibly some image loss, but in real estate, the potential to lose tens of thousands of dollars on any one deal is very real.

Most investors and online gurus overlook the less glamorous aspects of flipping like properly evaluating a deal, surrounding yourself with the right people to make it flow seamlessly, all the things that could go wrong, and some contingency options to make sure you don't lose your shirt. The overarching piece of advice here is to never jump into your first flip by yourself unless you are a contractor, home inspector, or some other form of highly qualified professional. Partner up on a deal or two by finding others with capital and expertise to provide an extra set of eyes on everything and create a safety net in case something does go wrong – trust me, it will.

Deal Evaluation

Evaluating the profitability of flip deals is a completely different animal than any other type of real estate investment, mainly because there is only one exit strategy. If any component of your estimates from the after-renovation value to the individual line items on the repair list is wrong, you can quickly find yourself in a situation where the finished product is worth less than what you have invested. When this happens, you are left with two distinctly unappealing options: sell it at a loss or hold on to the property and try renting it in some way to stem the bleeding. The good news is, as long as you follow the steps outlined for evaluating deals and having contingency plans, none of those outcomes should apply.

By far the most important component of deal evaluation is calculating the after-renovated value of the property. Notice the word "calculating," not determining, estimating, or figuring. Too many people assume they know what properties are worth because they base it off their own home price, listen to the chatter from friends and neighbors, or do a quick Zillow search and automatically use the highest-priced homes in an area to base their numbers on. I can't even say one of these strategies is better than the others because they are all equally horrible, subjective, and bound to get you in trouble. The only way to confidently get an idea of what a particular home might sell for is to perform a comparative market analysis (CMA), preferably with the assistance of a licensed realtor who will access sales data you do not have access to.

A comparative market analysis takes many market factors into account to make sure the estimated value is as close to what you can realistically expect upon sale as possible. The first criterion in a CMA would be the geographic proximity of other homes sold in the area. If investing in a population-dense market like NYC or LA, the rule of thumb would be to only use comparable sales within a quarter mile of where your flip project is located. If the market is more suburban, such as on the outskirts of a major city, the search radius can be extended out to half a mile or up to a maximum of one mile. If you're flipping in a very rural area, it won't be uncommon to need a search area of two-plus miles to get enough data – although these markets can be the most dangerous because of low population, which generally indicates less demand. No matter which scenario describes your market, make sure to use the lower end of the average home value in the CMA to ensure you are not only looking at the best-case scenario.

Get Real!

One exception to the CMA radius rule would be when comparable properties in the approved radius have other material differences from your subject property characteristics like zip codes, school districts, and city or county lines, which can all render a nearby property ineligible to be used as a valid comparable sale. It is not uncommon for properties located on opposite sides of a street to have varying values because of the previously mentioned factors. People don't just buy homes – they buy everything that home can provide them above and beyond shelter: schools, public services, and other amenities. The deal in question could be larger and more appealing on the surface than other comparable sales across the street or around the corner, but if it is zoned for a different public school or does not have access to the town pool or beach, the value will be negatively impacted. That is why it is so important to work with a knowledgeable professional who knows all these intricacies until you learn the ropes, and even then, you should still have these professionals in your back pocket.

To some degree, the type of home needs to be factored in as well since not all construction types are created equal in every market. It is fairly well-known that two-family homes generally have a lower price per square foot than single-family homes, and three-family homes are lower than both. However, there can also be price adjustments for raised ranch homes compared to colonial homes or brick homes versus A-frame houses. A good rule of thumb is to get a feel for what the most popular type of construction is in a particular area and invest in similar-looking properties. Having the unique property – for better or worse – in the neighborhood may be fine when you plan to live there long term, but when the goal is for a quick sale, it is best to have a home most of the population seems to prefer in your desired area.

We also need to tackle the question of having the largest or smallest house. Generally, CMAs look at homes that fall within 300-600 square feet of one another for estimation purposes. Much like we mentioned earlier about some upgrades being so extravagant that the owner can never hope to recover the investment, a house twice the size of the average is going to yield a lower price per square foot than its smaller neighbors. Believe it or not, a house that is much smaller than its average neighbors will often yield a higher price per square foot, so long as it is in decent condition. There is no hard and fast rule for determining the adjustments on a national level, but a qualified realtor or appraiser in your market can give you a better understanding of how they work.

Almost as important as the type of home and where it is located would be the average time a home in a particular area sits on the market before going into contract. This can give you a pretty good idea of how long you can expect to get your money after renovations are complete. These numbers can change drastically and often, so it is advisable to stay on top of local trends. If the average time on the market when you close on a property is six weeks, that needs to get added to your overall timeline after your renovation schedule. So, an eight-week renovation project would likely then need another six weeks on the market before it goes into contract. Then, you have to account for the time it takes to get from contract to closing, which could be another four to eight weeks. This is incredibly important because you need to make sure your profitability calculations allow for paying all necessary property expenses for almost six months.

Pitfalls

It should be no surprise to find an entire section dedicated to the most common pitfalls investors make when getting involved with flip projects. That's not to say flip investing is any riskier than other areas of real estate, but it usually comes with only one exit strategy, and time is of the essence, so every day eats away at your profits. The good news is, my partners and I have made just about every mistake you (or we) can think of and hope to help you avoid doing the same by giving you the good, the bad, and the ugly up front.

Almost all the pitfalls we will discuss in this section revolve around time – how quickly you can get the repairs done, how quickly you can get permits closed, and how long it will take to find a buyer. The one factor, and arguably one of the most minimized by new investors who have watched a few YouTube videos or paid for expensive online classes, is your own level of construction knowledge. If you are about to get offended and start rattling off all the reasons you are qualified – stop. Most people who get involved in flipping do have some level of knowledge or a desire to learn more; otherwise, this would not be the career path to take. But, a little bit of knowledge can be a dangerous thing.

To be quite honest, I am a perfect example. As a licensed real estate broker, I have been a part of countless transactions and, in the process, an equal amount of home inspections. As an investor with two partners who are both Master Home Inspectors, I've participated in dozens more informal inspections when we evaluate our own deals. Despite all that firsthand experience, I will be the first to tell you I should never be allowed to make any decisions when it comes to the estimation of cost or complexity. My mind just doesn't work that way. As the numbers guy – and every deal needs a numbers guy – all I want to know is what they estimate the renovation costs to be. Left to my own devices, I would have easily screwed up numerous estimates because I have a tendency of assuming everything is cut and dry when calculating costs.

Nothing in construction and remodeling is cut and dry though. I am going to repeat that, and please read it as many times as you need to. Nothing in construction and remodeling is cut and dry. The first place people go wrong with this belief is by assuming a project will be nothing more than "slapping lipstick on a pig," a creative real estate way of describing cosmetic surgery. There will be certain instances where money can be made by only performing surface-level enhancements like painting, flooring, appliances, and curb appeal. However, most savvy investors are all looking for easy deals like this, and once the bidding begins, the potential profit margins shrink, leaving the ultimate winner of the war with the lowest possible return.

With great risks come great rewards, and in real estate, the transformation process of a house has a special kind of allure. It takes equal parts vision and skill to see the hidden potential in older rundown houses and not only restore them to their former glory but also to adapt them to the current market trends. What was popular or appealing in a house from the 1920s will likely not be as attractive today, except to a very small segment of the market. Living situations have changed, construction and decor have transformed, and we have become programmed to keep up with the Joneses, which means having the shiniest new toys and features.

This is where the opening of Pandora's box is most likely to separate the skilled flippers from the novices who are in way over their heads. The second you open a wall or ceiling in a home, the potential for complications grows exponentially. I could write an entire book on all the different situations you might encounter, and even that would not be exhaustive, so for the purpose of this book, we can look at some of the most obvious ones. In fact, this exact scenario just happened to us on a renovation project for a property we intended to keep as a rental.

When we bought it, we knew the roof was shot. We knew with almost certain accuracy what the cost would be for a new roof and the approximate timeline for completion based on our contractor's schedule. This was a fairly routine project considering the three other houses we replaced roofs on in the last six months, or at least that was what we thought. Once the roofers started tearing off the old shingles, it quickly became apparent that the plywood under the roof was rotten due to excessive water damage. But, there were no visible signs of water damage inside the house that might have raised a red flag on the inspection. So, we opened up the ceiling on the top floor to discover that the entire wood frame, joists, rafters, and support beams were covered in mold.

Mold is one of those buzzwords in real estate that scares many away. Depending on who you talk to, the process for mold remediation can be as invasive as replacing all of the affected areas. This might not sound so extreme since there are numerous health issues associated with mold, and no one in their right mind should ever ignore the presence of mold once they know it is there, no matter how much or little. What most don't know though is there are much cheaper and easier ways to treat the problem with the same level of effectiveness – because the remediation industry does not want you to know a few gallons of mold-killing spray and a coat of Kilz paint will accomplish the same thing for a fraction of the cost. Knowing what we do, we were fortunate to avoid the hefty cost some would have paid, but we still lost time and money in treating it before the ceilings could be closed again.

What else could go wrong? Maybe your vision calls for removing a wall in the kitchen to create an open concept, but you find out after the demolition starts that there is plumbing or electric wiring in the wall that now needs to be relocated. It could be a question of upgrading the appliances and lighting in the house only to realize the existing electrical panel is not able to support the new load. That unfinished basement looked like a great way of adding extra square footage and living space, but the bathroom you wanted to create down there was below the main plumbing line and now a booster pump is needed at a significant increase in cost. If you are still wondering what could go wrong with your particular project, just use your imagination.

All the scenarios above will cost you money, but they will also cost you time. Time is so valuable in home flipping, it is often advisable to pay more money for fixes just to get them done quicker. That is part of the reason we included determining the average time it takes for a home to sell, but there are also other time-bound concerns of equal importance that need to happen before you can even arrive at the point of selling. The one most often overlooked and potentially the most serious, depending upon where the project is located, is the time needed and cost associated with getting building department permits to begin the renovations and scheduling the inspections needed to certify the work.

Many remodelers prefer to bypass the permit process, and understandably so, but there are pros and cons on both sides of the argument. From a legal standpoint, if the local municipality requires permits for the work you are doing, then you should know in advance how long the process takes and the cost associated with it. From a practical standpoint, there are certain instances where you can risk bypassing the process. In a place like NYC, it is almost never advisable to skip any permits because of the monetary fines associated with getting caught and the overall delay to your project. Once the building department finds out work is being performed without a permit (it is always a neighbor who rats you out), the project is shut down until all fines are paid, proper permits are issued, and inspectors can sign off on the work completed to date – which, in many instances, might require cutting walls back open at your expense.

In more suburban or rural areas, the building departments are less stringent, and you likely have fewer neighbors looking to cause you trouble. Just make sure you are aware of your surroundings, but that doesn't mean it is a foolproof option to avoid filing. Embarrassingly enough, we recently had a project shut down because we did not file for permits, assuming we would never get caught, but we failed to realize one key piece of information. In fact, for weeks, we could not figure out how the local building inspector in a city of less than 4,000 people found out we were gut renovating an apartment. We were sure one of the other tenants in the building filed a complaint out of spite since they were in the process of being evicted for nonpayment. After a casual conversation with the inspector who came to sign off on the work, it turned out we were caught because of our own stupidity. The local building department was housed in the building directly across the street from our property, and he watched with his own eyes as a truckload of construction materials was delivered. Thankfully, it was small-town America, and we avoided any penalties and only suffered a slight delay.

While we are not advocating for you to proceed one way or another, a good rule of thumb to apply if you are weighing whether or not to pull permits is to know what types of repairs can come back to bite you when it is time to sell. You might remember from Chapter 1 that any modifications affecting the property footprint or room number are bound to come up on a title search. If permits were not filed, you are now stuck in a situation where the buyer will face complications with their bank, thus limiting your pool of potential suitors. By virtue of supply and demand, having less qualified buyers will negatively impact your resale value and cause the house to sit on the market longer than it would have otherwise.

Other holding costs to be aware of are included in the deal evaluation calculator but are important enough to call them out here as pitfalls as well. Property taxes are generally only paid two or three times a year, a portion of which is prepaid at closing. When your project runs into the next tax cycle, you will need the cash on hand to cover the expense. Utility bills can also start to add up as you will need electricity to power equipment, heat to ensure pipes don't freeze, air conditioning to accommodate laborers in the summer, and water. If you didn't pay cash, the cost of your loan is another important consideration, not just the monthly payment.

Many rehabilitation loans come with a short-term balloon payment, meaning you must sell or refinance the property before the end of the term. Depending on the lender, these terms can vary from 6-18 months, but don't take the time for granted. When the balloon payment comes due, the lender will foreclose on the house if you are unable to restructure the loan. Then, there are the closing costs on the sale of the home to consider as well as taxes. Between attorneys, realtors, and other transfer costs, you could easily be looking at thousands of additional dollars in sunk costs, and no amount of planning can ever guarantee everything goes in your favor.

We had the good fortune of picking up a parcel of land that contained three individual homes, all in need of varying renovations, for about $200k under what we believed the properties to be worth once restored to their former glory. Before making an offer, the property was inspected by our home inspectors, so we thought we had a fairly good idea of what we would need to spend on renovations. That was until we tore down the sheetrock on the ceiling to discover an abundance of mold no one could have known was there. After ripping open some walls, we found massive plumbing damage that, again, could not be detected on an inspection since, as we said earlier, it is non-invasive.

Then, we got to the logistics of estimating material, ordering it, and scheduling delivery. Having dozens of completed flips under our belts, this is generally a routine and mundane part of the process. That was until our supplier, who shall not be named for legal reasons, shipped 2,000 square feet of the wrong flooring to our job site. We were not on-site because we had a contracting crew there to receive the shipment and start the work. The foreman sent us a picture and called us to ask why the flooring delivered did not match the rest of the house. Well, because the supplier goofed up! Rather than rectify it, the supplier wanted us to bring it all back to the warehouse for exchange. This led to hours wasted on the phone trying to schedule the return and sparked a dispute with the foreman who refused to load the material back onto the van once the supplier agreed to send it back because it was "not his job." After another couple of hours wasted to resolve that dispute, the entire day was gone without anything accomplished. Are you getting the point as to how it does not have to be one major issue that throws a project off schedule? Sometimes, a few smaller issues can be far worse.

If any or all of these pitfalls scare you – good. Knowledge is power. Going into a transaction fully aware of all the potential complications is like going through the side effects of a medicine with your doctor or preparing for potential complications from surgery. It is only when things come as a complete surprise that we stand to lose money. It can feel hopeless and overwhelming when the unexpected happens, which means you must prepare to expect anything and everything. I would rather be in a position of needing to figure out which contingency plan to activate as opposed to creating those plans on the fly when the clock is ticking and money is dripping.

Contingency Plans

Most of us do not plan to fail, and we probably do not even fail to plan. Where we do run into problems is in assuming the one and only plan we created at the outset of a project is going to be the one we stick with all the way to closing. This is an admirable mindset since the last thing one would want to do is go into a project with too many potential outcomes and not enough focus on any of them, but it can also lead to disappointment when Plan A doesn't work out. In flip investing, Plan A is almost always selling the property at a profit. Unfortunately, things do not always work out the way we plan for countless reasons. Markets cool down, more inventory becomes available and drives down prices, interest rates rise sharply, and the list goes on and on. So what happens when you find yourself sitting with a house that is not generating any income but still costs money every month to carry?

One of the most publicized strategies for building real estate portfolios is the BRRR method, which stands for Buy, Renovate, Refinance, and Repeat. Considering we have a multi-pronged strategy, this is not usually our default definition of success on a flip project, but in the event we are unable to find a buyer, using a bank to refinance it and possibly cash out some equity to use for more acquisitions is not a bad idea. The trick with falling back on this option is that the home must be profitable enough after the refinance so any rent received leaves you in the positive. Most will never even consider what the rent on a flip might be since they have no intention of holding it, but for those tight deals, it is definitely an option you should want to know early on if is viable.

The next creative strategy for when a house won't sell, and one we have successfully employed multiple times, is the rent-to-own scenario. What makes this an attractive option is the ability to charge a higher than FMR on the property while making it beneficial for the would-be owner. In these scenarios, the tenant is given a monthly rent amount, which consists of a portion that gets credited toward a down payment for a future purchase date and a pre-agreed purchase price as stipulated in the contract. We generally give the tenant two years before they must complete the purchase or forfeit all the extra money contributed toward the closing costs. Should they decide to purchase it sooner, they will receive full credit for any down payments received, and we can expedite the process.

This is a typical rent-to-own contract we recently completed:

Purchase Price: $120,000
FMR: $1,000/mo
Rent-to-own: $1,500/mo
Down payment credit: $500/mo
24-month down payment: $12,000

As you can see, these numbers have been engineered to benefit all parties. The additional rent payment every month will leave the buyer in a position to have a 10% down payment at the end of the term, which would qualify them for most mortgages. They now have the opportunity to purchase a home they might not have been able to afford otherwise and likely would not still be available two years in the future. We are making enough extra money per month to keep the property profitable and also know in two years' time, we will either get the remaining lump sum profit when they buy, or we will have the option of putting it back on the market while keeping the $12K should the buyer change their mind or be unable to qualify for a mortgage for whatever reason.

Airbnb and other short-term vacation rentals are another great opportunity when stuck with a profit-leaking property. Yes, there is more work and expense in doing this, but depending on how desirable your market is, these numbers can turn out more profitable than doing a standard rental or rent-to-own. The best part of this is you do not have to do anything high-end or fancy. Sure, if you happen to have a three-bedroom cabin in the woods, you might want to lean into the experience so you can charge slightly more per night, but if you have a tiny unit in the city, an air mattress, kitchen supplies, and an internet connection can do the trick.

A few years back, I owned a small two-family house in the suburbs right outside of NYC. Because it was expensive to hold and the rents were well over $2K per unit, it only took one unit being vacant for me to lose money. After a long-term tenant moved out and I could not rent the tiny one-bedroom unit for what I needed, I went the Airbnb route. I also took it a step further and replaced the living room with another bedroom. Someone could rent the entire apartment for around $100/night or by room for $55/night. Once I worked out all the logistics, it was booked more than 20 nights a month and brought in more profit than when I had long-term tenants in place.

Another creative option is to find out what housing the local community needs. Because of our relationship with Section 8 and the county's Human Services office, we found out these organizations often pay local motels to offer temporary housing to people who are awaiting more permanent solutions. What better way to fill a community need and keep some cash flow coming in than by offering up your vacant units as an option for their temporary and overflow housing needs? Where there is a will, there is always a way. Doing anything is better than just sitting back and hoping for the best.

"Real estate investing, even on a very small scale, remains a tried and true means of building an individual's cash flow and wealth."

— Robert Kiyosaki

Chapter 8: Wholesaling

Wholesaling in real estate has become one of the hottest trends over the last couple years, so much so that everyone and anyone on Facebook and other social media platforms is offering master classes, webinars, and private coaching on it. It has become such a buzzword that many folks who are new to real estate don't even realize how many other ways there are to make money besides playing the middleman in a wholesaling transaction. Like every other investment strategy, with real estate being no exception, there are benefits and pitfalls to focusing only or too heavily on wholesaling.

Before we can even dive into the nitty gritty details of wholesaling, let's first make sure we understand exactly what the process looks like. In a typical real estate transaction, a buyer goes into a contract with a seller, and those two parties take the contract all the way through to execution – where the buyer takes possession of the property. In wholesaling, the original buyer is really only a buyer in name. Their purpose is to get the property under contract so they can then turn around and assign the contract to another buyer, who will take the contract to execution. The original buyer will hopefully already have a buyer lined up to avoid any potential losses, which we will cover later, but for illustrative purposes, here is how a typical wholesaling deal would play out:

- John Smith identifies a property he believes is undervalued or can be negotiated down to a price where he can then sell it for more.
- John Smith makes an offer of $200K for said property, and the contract reads: John Smith and/or assigns.
- John Smith finds a buyer willing to pay $220K for the property he has in contract and "assigns" the contract to the new buyer.
- As long as the deal makes it to closing, John Smith makes $20K on the deal without ever having to take possession of the property.

This book is not meant to be a master class on wholesaling or walk anyone through the entire process, but rather to illustrate the way it works so you can make an informed decision as to how it works. The key item to take away from the example above to really understand whether or not this can be completed successfully on any given deal is the use of the phrase "and/or assigns." Many sellers and attorneys prefer not to see this wording, as it can complicate the transaction by requiring contracts to be amended with the new buyer's name and can add an element of uncertainty. Without that wording, there is no legally binding way to make the seller accept your assignment and collect the $20K profit instead of just canceling the deal with you and selling directly to the new buyer for the full $220K.

Finding deals in wholesaling is very much the same as the other avenues of real estate investing, but there is one additional avenue to consider if you are new to the business. By affiliating yourself with an existing wholesaling operation, which are generally the ones bragging about how great this business is on social media in an attempt to get you on board, you can cut out a lot of the leg work. They already have lists of potential prospects, proven scripts to use, and the capital needed to put deals under contract so you do not have to take any risk. This can sound attractive to many starting out, and depending on your knowledge and commitment levels, it is not necessarily a bad way to start out. The downside here is no risk equals no reward. The typical wholesaling shop might pay out 10%-35% of the money made on the entire transaction while they keep the rest, but again, 100% of 0 is 0.

Benefits

There are many legitimate benefits to justify wholesaling as a real estate investment option. The premise is the same as what happens in any retail store in the world. The merchant purchases their inventory from a wholesaler in bulk and then charges a higher price to sell it to the general public. Some wholesalers claim to do dozens of deals every month, while others are lucky if they can manage one or two per quarter because much like other areas of real estate, the technique is *simple,* but it is not *easy.*

One of the main reasons wholesaling gets so much attention on social media is that there is a very low barrier to entry when it comes to capital requirements and technical knowledge. Find an undervalued property and bring it to a buyer who recognizes the real value – simple, right? It is, but it takes dedication and persistence to make hundreds of phone calls or knock on dozens of doors every month. Home sellers are not lining up in droves in search of wholesalers when they are ready to list. They are either listing as an FSBO or contacting a real estate agent in the hopes of getting top dollar.

As a wholesaler, you must differentiate yourself from all the other investors trying to separate a homeowner from their property. The best way to do that is by focusing on how quick and easy you can make the process for them. Thinking back to the chapters on buying and selling, the highest price is not always the main factor in a person's decision, especially for those who know their property may have some issues or a lack of buyers interested in buying it in its present state.

Remember, you must have the cash on hand to put the house into contract. In some markets, like New York City or Los Angeles, most serious sellers are looking for a minimum of 10% down payment at contract signing, which can add up to tens of thousands of dollars. In other rural markets where we also invest quite successfully, many sellers are happy or naive enough to accept $1K-$5K as a down payment in the hopes of getting rid of the property quickly. These numbers are important to know because they will give you a baseline for just how many deals you can attempt to wholesale at one time. $50K in the bank may only give you enough for one down payment in a major metropolitan area, yet get you ten in areas less in demand.

Because of the low capital requirements, the potential for turning quick profits is another major reason investors and would-be real estate tycoons get into the world of wholesaling. To truly reap the rewards of potentially turning a quick profit on a small capital investment, chances are, you will need to broker several wholesale deals per month to support yourself as a full-time real estate investor. Even if you make $10K-$20K per deal, there are soft costs that must be accounted for. You may have to pay for marketing or lead generation to acquire the clients, the government is going to want estimated income taxes every quarter based on your earnings, and you will need to keep cash in the bank to keep funding new deals while waiting for other deals to get assigned or closed.

Lastly, one of the most unsung benefits of wholesaling is not having to deal with the entire closing process. Yes, you will likely still need to wait until closing to get paid, unless you have worked out an arrangement with the buyer allowing you to recoup your down payment on assignment, but the new buyer will be the one dealing with all of the activities and headaches required to reach a closing table. Unless you are a control freak who needs to be involved in everything – in which case, this would be the wrong strategy for you anyway – you can immediately start focusing on landing your next deal while waiting for a check from the prior deal.

Pitfalls

Just because your role in a wholesaling transaction is more of a middleman or conduit bringing together buyers and sellers does not mean no risk exists. In fact, so many people underestimate the potential dangers in wholesaling, and that is the exact reason we need to be that much more vigilant. The dollars at risk might be much less than in other real estate activities, but losing them will hurt all the same. Going into wholesaling with the mentality that it is quick and easy money is the best way to get yourself in trouble. The goal of wholesaling is to get as many deals into contract as quickly as possible to achieve the crazy returns those gurus advertise.

However, making decisions quickly in real estate is kind of like throwing darts at a board when deciding which stocks to buy. You may get one right here and there, but will the amount made outweigh all the times you get it wrong? This all starts with market knowledge. As a new real estate investor, you might not even know enough about the market you live in, let alone nationwide. Making hundreds of calls every day to potential sellers can leave you jaded and mentally exhausted. When you finally get someone on the phone who expresses interest, there is a tendency to feel the need to make the deal work, to refill your tank by getting success under your belt. This overeagerness to make a deal work can lead to overpaying, which will quickly limit your pool of potential assignees for the contract.

This brings us to the next potential pitfall, which is everything related to assignment issues with the contract. Remember, your only role in this type of deal is to connect a seller and buyer, but you are using your money to do it. Even if you bought at the right price, there still needs to be a buyer to complete the transaction. If you have not given serious thought to who you are going to pitch these deals to before laying out money, then you might be in for a rude awakening. Think about some of these questions:

- How many buyers do you have?
- How well do you know them?
- Have you verified their ability to take the contract?
- Proof of funds
- Pre-approval
- Do they have a track record with others you know well?
- How many deals have they passed up in the last 12 months?

Keep all these questions in mind before ever picking up a telephone. If you don't know the answers to these questions, make getting them a top priority. If any of the potential investors you plan on assigning contracts to are offended by these questions, the problem is with them, not you. Any legitimate investor should appreciate you taking the time to perform due diligence so no one's time is wasted. In wholesaling, you truly are only as good as your last deal. Since you retain no ownership interest in anything, your reputation is one of the most important things you can bring to the table. Be wary of anyone or anything that sounds too good to be true, and always exercise caution before signing any contract, especially before remitting any earnest money to solidify that contract.

"Risk comes from not knowing what you're doing."

— Warren Buffett

Chapter 9: Cautionary Situations

You might have caught on by now to the fact that as rewarding as real estate can be, it also comes with the potential for significant risk. Some of those risks are unavoidable; they can be minimized and mitigated but not entirely eliminated. Other risks are completely avoidable if you know what to look for. Sometimes, the very thing you think will be the factor working in your favor turns out to be the biggest mistake you could possibly make. The more time you dedicate to your real estate avenue of choice, the better you will get at learning to identify these potential areas early on, then trust your gut to avoid falling victim to them.

Partners

One of the biggest areas to exercise caution is with partners. The thought of going into business with other people can oftentimes sound attractive to those new to real estate since they will likely lack capital, experience, or both. Finding a partner who knows more about the industry or who has access to capital or credit can surely speed up the learning curve and get you making money sooner, but it can also lock you into an unhealthy relationship that is not easy to exit. Think of it like a bad marriage where divorce is not an option. Remember, real estate is not a liquid asset and can not be sold quickly in the event of a falling out with a business partner.

That's not to say you should avoid partners at all costs though. Every successful partnership consists of several key areas. Being aware of what they are will allow you to have clear and specific conversations with any potential business partner, whether they are actively involved in the daily operations or are just a silent investor lending money for you to manage. One of the worst things you can do in any business, but especially in real estate, is assume you and your partners are 100% on the same page. Experience has taught me that if you were to ask a current or prospective business partner to write down the top three to five objectives they have from the business and then compare it with your same list, not only will you find you are not on the same page, but it is likely you are not even reading the same book!

With that said, never enter into any type of partnership without clearly defining the goals of said arrangement. If one partner is looking to achieve a passive income of "x dollars" per month to supplement their retirement income, and the other partner is looking to cash out a lump sum in the next three months to pay for a family vacation, chances are, one or both will be left unhappy. Maybe one partner is much more risk averse than the other and is happy to achieve overall returns in the 8% range, while the other partner considers anything less than 12% to be a waste of time. Don't even think about what happens when there is a third or fourth partner involved!

Should both partners be looking for the same result, in this case, let's say it is to achieve a certain amount of passive income, but one wants to do it with commercial real estate while the other wants to use multifamily residential, problems are still bound to arise. This is why, beyond making sure all partners have the same goals, it is crucial to make sure everyone is in alignment with the ways of achieving those goals. It can be easy to think all profit is created equal and any deals that help you reach the overall goals should be considered. This may not mean needing to define each investment objective to a granular level, but setting parameters will be helpful. In our business model, we have defined metrics for what makes a flip deal viable and then very different ones for cash flow investing. We know what property types we want, the geographic location down to zip codes, and the maximum purchase price. Sure, a deal will come up every once in a while that does not fit neatly into any of our boxes, but that is where all partners vote on whether it is something worth pursuing or not. If the vote ends in a tie, someone is going to have to give.

One of the quickest ways for a partnership to go south is when one party feels like they are contributing more than another. This is another area that is easy enough to handle early on by outlining the responsibilities and expectations for each partner. If the intent is to split everything 50/50, then both partners need to bring the same amount of cash to the table and be willing to commit the same amount of time to run the business. If one partner has all the capital, then the other will likely need to put in more time on the operations to make it equitable. Once that is determined, the partners can then decide who is going to be responsible for which aspects of the operations. In our business, each of the three of us has very defined roles based on our area of expertise. For example, I handle the finances, one partner handles the tenant relations, and the third coordinates our partnerships and vendor relationships. Occasionally, we will cross into one another's territory, but that person will always have the final say.

Exit strategies and generational planning are not always something those of the younger generation tend to focus on upfront. We tend to believe we are immortal and have all the time in the world to accomplish our goals. The hard truth of it is, none of us are promised tomorrow. If you step outside tomorrow and get hit by a truck, what happens to your stake in the real estate partnership? Many just assume that their business partner will take care of their family, or if their children are old enough, they will just step in and take over. Neither of those goes very far in the way of peace of mind, which is why we mentioned buy-sell agreements in Chapter 1. I know in my personal business, should I die tomorrow, my children are too young to take over, my wife has no interest in real estate, and my partners would be stuck with the burden of doing my job as well as theirs. Having a plan on paper and an insurance policy to support it while you live to 100 years old is a far better position to be in than having no plan in place and leaving your loved ones in a tough situation.

It is also advisable to understand who you are dealing with before ever thinking about entering into a formal partnership. There is no right or wrong answer here, just awareness above all else. Many people will tell you business and family don't mix, while others will swear family are the only ones you can trust not to steal from you. The same can be said for silent partners, experienced partners, licensed partners, and the list goes on. The only thing that really matters here is knowing as much about them as possible. Too many times, investors will get into relationships with a partner without realizing their partner has other partners behind them who they are also accountable to. Can you see where this might get convoluted?

Affiliated Business Relationships

Another red flag in the real estate world is affiliated business relationships. Everyone likes to say they know someone. "I've got a guy," is often the exact phrase you will hear, and there is nothing inherently wrong with that. As a real estate professional, "I've got a guy" for just about everything you can imagine. I don't push those relationships on my clients or partners, but they are good to have as options. In an industry where time kills deals and teamwork is of paramount importance, I want to know I have a myriad of options for my clients. This means giving the names of three home inspectors, mortgage brokers, attorneys, or any other professional service provider. If the client does not want to interview all three and asks for my recommendation, I will give it and explain why. If they have their own providers, I will never push mine but will absolutely stress the expectations I will have of them.

This is a very different approach from many who will try to force you to use their provider of choice. When a listing agent insists on their mortgage broker reviewing any pre-approval documents, due diligence borders on unethical. It is understandable to want to work with someone who you know gets the job done, but the buyer and their agent now must question where the allegiance of the mortgage broker lies. The same thing applies when pushing to use their preferred inspector or attorney. Even though these professionals all have legal and ethical responsibilities to the person they represent and not the one who referred them, sadly, there are horror stories all the time. Just think back to my story from the introduction, where my partner and I worked with an agent who was handling multiple aspects of the sale. His promise of simplicity and having everything handled for me was enticing enough to lure me in, but it wasn't until after the sale that I found out everyone was working together to help their client offload properties on an unsuspecting third party – me!

Dual Agency

The dual agency realtor is another relationship that should set off alarms in your mind. Too many agents like to brag about how they do most of their deals in-house with other agents on their team or wind up with both sides of the deal themselves, representing both the buyer and seller. What's interesting about this is that it is legal in all states I know of, and one of the only positions in a real estate transaction where it is acceptable. But it wouldn't make much sense to have the same attorney represent both sides, so it sure doesn't with realtors either. It is just not possible to always equally represent the best interest of a buyer and seller, especially when there are points of negotiation. The agent representing both sides stands to make double the commission on the sale and will often give preference to buyers without an agent so they can claim that double dip.

I once worked with a broker in my early days of being licensed who proudly boasted that in the prior year, 97% of his deals were "doubleheaders," where he represented both sides of the transaction. As a rookie, that sounded impressive, but it did not take long to see how he achieved that metric and the harm it did to his clients. When it came time to evaluate deals, he would guide his sellers to lower-priced offers or ones with less advantageous terms if those buyers did not have an agent. In certain instances, he would go out of his way to make it difficult for another agent to cooperate or even sabotage deals so he could fall back on his own buyers at the expense of his clients' time and profit. Granted, he was a special case, and I like to think most agents would never make a practice of behaving like this, but the fact remains that these types of situations can blur the lines of ethical behavior.

Financial Health

The last red flag we want to pay attention to has nothing to do with anyone but yourself – and your credit score. When anyone gets into real estate for the first time, they are generally focused on, if not obsessed with, their credit score. The importance of having good credit is beaten into our heads because of the opportunity it affords, but what those same people fail to realize is that there is more to a good credit score than paying your bills on time. Each time you apply for a mortgage, or any form of credit for that matter, an inquiry is performed on your credit, and the score will drop. Each new loan you take out will also drop your credit score. These are not huge hits when looked at individually and are a necessary evil of doing business, but over time, the impact can add up to a dangerous level.

If you are buying one property on average a year, chances are, you will not experience an issue here. But, imagine for a moment you are buying one each quarter. That equates to four hits on your credit report every year along with four new loans. Where this can become dangerous is when you plan on having certain options available to you because of a stellar credit score, only to find out you have dropped below the acceptable minimum. In a best-case scenario, this might only cost you the opportunity of acquiring a new property, but in a worst-case scenario, you could find yourself with a balloon payment coming due and no way to refinance it. Always stay on top of your credit score to ensure you are financially healthy. Whether it be Credit Karma or any of the monitoring services offered for free through many banks and credit card companies, keeping an eye on your score every month allows you to identify negative trends early on and take corrective action before a sticky situation arises.

Occupied Property

In a perfect world, every property you buy, regardless of what your end goal is, will be vacant or delivered vacant. However, there can be tremendous opportunities in buying an occupied property. That's not to say it is for the faint of heart, but scared money doesn't make money. Whether it be your primary residence, a property you wanted to rent, or a flip, the likelihood of having an existing owner who is not ready to leave by closing or a tenant who refuses to leave for one reason or another is very real. The question is not how to avoid finding yourself in a situation with a holdover tenant, but rather how to handle those situations with the utmost tact and strategy so you can be profitable while staying on the right side of the law.

Sometimes, one of the best parts about buying occupied property is the additional insights you can gain into the condition of the home. It can be easy to overlook little details when a home is vacant because you do not expect to see evidence of how the prior owners were living. With multiple people living in a home – eating, bathing, and sleeping – there are certain things one would expect to see. Running water, functional appliances, and safe living conditions are just a few of those items. What kind of red flag would it set off for you if a bedroom door was padlocked and labeled "KEEP OUT" or if there was a network of garden hoses running throughout the house? Well, here's what it meant for us in one of the most humorous walk-throughs we ever conducted.

I was the first one to walk through a three-family rental property we were looking to buy (something I will be the first to say should never happen without supervision) and knew it was going to be a disaster from the start. The door to the main unit was partially blocked by a restaurant grade refrigerator/freezer unit on the porch. Once I squeezed past to get inside, I had to wonder why they would have a refrigerator that large and yet still keep bowls full of chicken feet (yep, just the feet) defrosting on the kitchen countertops. But hey, we were buying a house, not their lifestyle, right?

Making my way up to the second floor, I still did not grasp all the potential red flags from how the rooms were partitioned, although I got the feeling that way more people were living here than the septic system could probably handle. Those fears were instantly overshadowed by the bedroom door with the "KEEP OUT" scrawled across it in black Sharpie marker. I didn't think twice about going in since the realtor had the key but was quickly met with a beehive on the far side of the room that consumed the entire window. The listing agent and I took one look at each other, asked each other in unison if our eyes were playing tricks on us, then shut the door just as quickly as we had opened it when the buzzing started.

At this point, I didn't need to see any more of the house. Having been sending pictures and videos to my partners the entire time, a consensus was quickly made that we would be hard pressed to turn a profit on the house. I didn't even question the series of different colored hoses running all across the first floor of the house and down the basement stairs. So, a few months later when the price dropped significantly, my partners came back with me for a second attempt at justifying the purchase. Equally as intrigued by the hose situation as I was, they began tracing each of the lines into the basement, only to find they ran over a series of barrels and plastic drums filled with water, which then had spigots conveniently tapped into the hoses above each drum. It was like a low-tech science experiment we could not figure out – until we followed the hoses outside to the creek behind the house.

I was still baffled when the lightbulb went off for my partners. Apparently, they were siphoning water from the creek and using gravity to feed it into the house. This water was then combined along with repurposed waste water (think of the water that goes down any drain or toilet), storing this concoction of "fresh water" in the assorted barrels throughout the basement. This became a clear problem for several reasons. The first being it was not environmentally acceptable. The second, which was more their problem than ours, was that it is not hygienic. The third and biggest issue for us was that it indicated there was an issue with the well water on the property, signifying a potentially very expensive upgrade. Even though we passed on the house a second time, this feat of ingenuity still remains one of the most memorable homemade hacks to get running water I've ever seen.

Above profitability, speed, and convenience is the question of legality. When buying any property that will be delivered with occupants, the most important considerations are those pertaining to local laws. It makes no difference as to why they are there and when they got there, but all occupants are afforded the same legal protections as a rental tenant who is behind on payments would be. Before ever entering into a contract, determine who the holdover occupant will be and what circumstance is keeping them there. These answers are usually divided into owners and tenants who are not leaving because they are already delinquent on payments or are just trying to figure out where to go.

Let's start by looking at the generally easier scenario, where it is the owner or an owner of the property who won't be leaving. The nice thing here is you will generally know upfront why and have a rough time frame attached. Most often, the situations arise because the seller is in the process of buying another property or moving into other types of living arrangements like assisted living or moving in with a child. My investment company does not believe in letting a good deal go by because we cannot take full possession at closing. Situations like this will often make a seller more negotiable on the price or other terms of the deal in return for your willingness to allow the current tenants to stay after closing. The trick here is finding a happy medium where the seller feels they have peace of mind, and you have not signed an open invitation to stay as long as they want. Every situation is totally different, and each investor must structure deals that work for them financially. Our general rule of thumb, so long as we get the right purchase price, is to allow the current owner a free 30 days after closing with a contingency to stay an extra 60 days at a pre-agreed monthly rent amount that covers our carrying costs and a minimal profit.

This is exactly what happened with another recent deal we put together with the help of a local realtor who was trying to help a mother and daughter buy a new home. They had already found something they liked but could not move forward with making an offer because they needed to sell their current two-family home first. Normally, the realtor would just list the house and get paid on both transactions, but the conditions were deplorable. There was junk piled floor to ceiling in every room, the front yard was loaded with trash, and the structure needed substantial work. So, the realtor called us and asked if we would buy the place.

Even though we planned on holding this as a rental property after renovations, we were able to position it as a flip to one of our lenders who agreed to finance 100% of the purchase and renovation costs. The problem was that the mother and daughter would not be able to close on their new home for at least 30 days after they sold it to us, and they had nowhere to go. In return for getting the price we wanted on the property, we offered a deal like what was just described, but not only did we allow them to stay rent-free until they could move, we also agreed to clean out all the trash and clutter at our expense. They still felt like they got less than the home was worth (they did not), but considering we were the only ones who would work with them, they ultimately realized there was no better option.

Sometimes, the owner/occupant is not a willing participant in the sale, and this is in most of the cases of contentious sales (estate, divorce, etc.), when other owners have made the decision to sell without the owner/occupant buy-in, or in a short sale or foreclosure situation, where the bank has initiated the transaction. Before you can go finding a solution, you will need to understand the real reason why someone won't leave.

Let's look at one of the most common situations, which is when an adult child of an elderly owner won't leave after the owner has died or has been relocated. Generally, there are multiple children involved in these decisions, and it is only the one living in the property who dissents to the sale and is now staying on principle. While you could use one of the strategies we will go into shortly, the best way of handling it is to try and have the sellers who are in agreement talk sense into their sibling and guarantee you in the contract that the house will be delivered vacant at closing. A similar approach would be advisable in divorce situations since the courts are overseeing the home sale and will have specific wording included in the settlement that ensures both parties fulfill the sale in good faith.

The last group of people, and by far the most complicated to deal with, are tenants who have been living there for a significant period of time - the longer they've been there, the harder it is to get them to leave. Chances are, they are paying far under fair market rent (FMR), have had free reign over the property, and are used to walking all over the current owner or landlord. The current landlord or owner might have just been too nice or timid to do what needed to be done, and that's the reason they are selling in the first place. No matter which of these options applies to your soon-to-be holdover tenants, the current owner is highly unlikely to help you get them out and will play stupid as to what your intentions are up to the very day of the sale. This is where local laws are going to be your best friend or worst enemy by dictating the best way to handle negotiations. No matter which strategy you choose to employ, it is always important to calculate no rent for the legal maximum amount of time it could take to get them out in your profitability calculations.

One of the most conservative strategies would be to play the nice guy upfront and play the game with them. Agree to let them stay for a few months at their current rent, or a slight increase, while everyone figures out their next move. This could quickly become a losing proposition for you though without a long-term plan for reaching your desired end state. If it is a flip, do you have work that can be done to other parts of the property while they continue living there? Renovations to other apartments and exterior spaces can help make the rest of the property start generating income to offset the loss on the unit with a holdover tenant.

This strategy of negotiating with the tenants is much more viable if they have been paying their rent on time to the previous owner. Sometimes, landlords just get sick of playing the collection agent every month and decide to sell simply to no longer have the headache. If that's the case with your tenant, it might be worth trying to negotiate. However, if you negotiate with tenants who are known for not paying their rent on time or have been known to cause problems, you will likely have to listen to and agree with all the grievances they air against their prior owner in justification of why they have not been paying their rent. Just realize that any deal struck through this type of negotiation strategy will soon have you becoming the villain in their story and rent payments disappearing again. Don't take anything at face value and make sure to collect the current month's rent to buy some breathing room before having to renegotiate.

Another more costly short-term strategy that can pay dividends in the long term is making a deal with the devil. Chances are, if they have a history of not paying rent, it is going to be difficult for them to find a new place to live. Landlords want references, and that generally includes an endorsement from their current landlord as well as the first month's rent and security deposit to secure the new place. It is not uncommon for new owners to incentivize a bad holdover tenant to leave by offering to pay their first month's rent and security deposit to expedite how quickly they become someone else's problem. This may also come with providing them with a reference, which could push your moral compass if you don't want to lie. It is not something I like to make a habit of, but I will admit there have been instances when I justified providing that reference to get them out of my property.

That last statement is the case-in-point argument for why I also fully subscribe to a "don't trust anyone mentality" and believe everyone should properly screen tenants prior to signing them on. Simply speaking to a person who claims to be the current landlord or certifies the rent is paid is not nearly enough for peace of mind. People lie when they need to, and it is much easier for people to do it without thinking twice over the phone to someone they've never met. Putting that same statement in writing in the form of an estoppel, a legal written certification attesting to current rent payments, will usually make someone think twice about lying. I would even go a step further and request the current landlord provide 12 months of canceled checks or other proof of timely payments. Ultimately, people can and still will lie, but every additional layer you add will make most people think twice about doing so to you.

One other creative option we have used to varying degrees of success is in helping the delinquent tenant get some type of assistance. The COVID-19 pandemic gave rise to one of the most recognizable assistance programs in the Emergency Rental Assistance Program (ERAP) than the real estate industry has ever seen before, but many similar programs have always existed on a smaller scale. You just need to know where to find them. In the last year, we have received rental assistance payments from organizations such as The Salvation Army, Catholic Charities of NEPA, VIP, Human Services, and several others. The only thing generally required from you, as the landlord, is a signed affidavit stating how much rent is past due and a guarantee that you will not evict the tenant if the payment is made. Oftentimes, these payments only serve as a bandage on a gunshot wound, but continuing to bring in cash flow is almost always better than trying to deal with the courts.

Now that we've covered all the possible ways of making a bad situation better, it deserves mentioning what you cannot do. It's a sad fact of real estate life, but your tenants, paying or not, have rights and legal protections – in some markets even more than the owner of the property. If you are currently responsible for paying the tenants' utilities, you cannot cease doing so regardless of their payment status. Even if you are suffering financial hardships as a result of their delinquency, the heat, hot water, and electricity must remain intact, or you can find yourself subject to civil and criminal penalties. You can also not do anything that would be considered harassment, which would include repeated phone calls or messages, calling before or after normal business hours, showing up unannounced, and so much more. Always keep in mind that tenants often know the laws better than their landlords and will go out of their way to make their lives miserable. Once they bring these counterclaims into a court proceeding, it can extend far longer than it might have otherwise and also wind up costing more money in the form of financial judgments against you.

As with every other chapter and section in this book, nothing is meant to scare you away from real estate, or in this case, properties with holdover tenants. There are tried and true ways of navigating these situations so you, the owner, have every opportunity of being successful and the tenants feel like they have been given a fair shake. The more leg work you can do before putting a property into contract, the better. Sometimes, the seller will facilitate having the conversation with their tenants, and other times, they will want no part of the drama. No matter which side of the coin you find yourself on, do as much research as possible and always trust your gut above all else.

A cautionary tale for why you should never trust anyone comes from a recent situation we encountered. We had a tenant pass away who was on public housing support. Her adult grandchild was living with her and had no place to go, prompting her to ask if she could pay us to rent privately until she found a new place. Having good hearts, we agreed, and everything went well for a few months until she suddenly stopped paying and responding. As it turned out, she had a major drug problem and moved her boyfriend in without our permission. So, after following the legal protocols and having her evicted, we were stunned when the marshall showed up to remove her, only to be informed that she was now out, but the boyfriend, whose name was not on any lease document, could not be removed because his name was not included in the eviction paperwork. Because of the technical loophole, we were stuck waiting another six weeks for the new proceedings and paperwork to take effect. The moral of the story – don't trust anyone, ever.

As you can see, there are many ways to lose money in real estate – some you will be responsible for, while others will be the work of opportunists trying to take advantage of you, your expertise, or your good nature. When you are always on guard and diligent in researching people to the same degree you do a potential property, the odds of success will be in your favor. When in doubt, use professional review sites like Zillow, Alignable, or Angie's List to qualify potential partners or service providers before entering into any deal or agreement. When possible, only work with those who come highly recommended by other experts in your field or circle. Above all else, and it can not be stated too many times, use common sense and trust your gut to eliminate most of the most common situations failed investors find themselves in.

"In my experience, in the real-estate business past success stories are generally not applicable to new situations. We must continually reinvent ourselves, responding to changing times with innovative new business models."

— Akira Mori

Chapter 10: Creative Options

Even though the physical appearance of real estate (land, houses, buildings, etc.) has not changed much over the years, it would be foolhardy to think prior investing strategies can remain static in an evolving world. This holds especially true in real estate, where more and more investors are looking to get involved every day, the amount of land available on Earth is finite, and the number of homes becoming available on a daily basis is limited. This fact can make many feel like there are no good deals available, only the big guys have a chance to compete, or any other countless excuses on why a career in real estate won't work.

However, there is a wide array of new options opening up every day. Think back a decade or two ago, when there was a limited number of options one had for renting out their home – find a long-term tenant or possibly rent out on a short-term basis to friends and family. Airbnb has changed that entire landscape. Now, when we have vacancies, we use their platform, in addition to other short-term rental sites and more traditional options. Using Airbnb quite literally made the difference in making one of my rental properties wildly profitable instead of the money pit it was prior.

To stay ahead of other investors with limited vision or an inability to adapt, do the opposite. Stay on top of market trends, read industry related news, and take note of what new options are becoming popular. Through our own investments and working with professional developers, we have compiled a list of the top six alternatives in real estate to the flipping, wholesaling, and multi-family rental options.

Tiny Homes

Much controversy surrounds the younger generations today and a perceived sense of entitlement or unwillingness to work hard. In reality, what has shifted is more mindset than work ethic. Younger people are looking at what their parents and grandparents worked a lifetime to achieve and are wondering if it is all worth it – big houses you hardly spend any time in, more cars than you possibly drive at a single time, and enough personal belongings to fill a storage facility. But for what?

Minimalistic living is making a comeback as prices increase and the desire for material possessions decreases. Tiny homes started a few years back as a fad many thought would never catch on. Now, there are more manufacturers and distributors jumping on the bandwagon than ever before. All you need is a small patch of land (or acreage if developing your own community), and your dream home can be delivered. If you decide you want a change of scenery down the road, you either have a smaller asset to sell, or you can pack it up and take it with you!

This is an area of the market to pay attention to going forward but not necessarily to dive in head first if you are inexperienced. Take a look at the companies specializing in the manufacturing of tiny homes and get an idea on pricing. Find others who are successfully doing it and pick their brains if possible. Rent one on Airbnb or a similar site for a night and immerse yourself in the experience. Note what you like and what you don't to incorporate into your own strategy when the time is right.

It is also important to realize many of the financing strategies we covered in Chapter 2 will not be applicable for these types of investments. The minimum loan amount most lenders will issue a mortgage on is $50K, so if your tiny home is less than that, you will need to look elsewhere. Also, most lenders require homes to have a "permanent foundation," disqualifying anything on wheels or not attached to a cement slab. Make sure you have designated lenders on your dream team who can assist here or enough of your own capital before setting your sights on this strategy.

Container Homes

This is another relatively new alternative to traditional living spaces catching on in ways most would not have believed. If you are unfamiliar with the trend, it is exactly what it sounds like. The containers used for shipping cargo on freight trains and ocean liners are now getting repurposed for living. If you still can't envision it, think about living in the back of a tractor-trailer. A used shipping container can be purchased online, with delivery included, for less than $10K depending on the condition. From there, the customization options are endless.

Depending on the municipality, the restrictions for making a shipping container a permanent residence may vary, but when done correctly, they are not much different from mobile or manufactured homes. But it takes vision, dedication, and know-how to pull it off. With access to the same qualified professionals needed to build or renovate a home (electricians, plumbers, carpenters, etc.), the finished product on a shipping container project would leave most hard-pressed to tell the difference between it and a traditional ranch-style home.

There are some stunning examples of what can be done with container homes on websites like Pinterest – or just Google it. With the right amount of work and vision, it can be nearly impossible to tell the finished product was ever a shipping container. In fact, as this trend continues growing, the options are getting more and more sophisticated. Some companies offer fully-built container homes, although the premium charged often makes it a less attractive option than tiny homes. And if you think the space is too small or restrictive, there is always the option of buying multiple containers, even of assorted sizes, and putting them together to form a container mansion!

Financing will also be an issue in the container home space though. If you happen to be purchasing a completed one where the owner has it affixed to a slab and the purchase price is over the $50K mortgage minimum, then banks might still be an option. But the real value is in creating these homes yourself to save money and accumulate equity, which means starting with raw land and a construction plan. Virtually no lenders will finance vacant land, so you need to plan for paying for that somehow. From there, construction loans, where a lender agrees to provide the capital in stages, might be an option. Each time you complete a phase of the project, the bank will inspect the progress and approve payments to your contractors so they can move on to the next phase.

Glamping

While the activity of glorified camping, or glamping, is not a specific real estate strategy, the opportunities it provides are. Traditional camping usually involves campgrounds, which can either be in a public or national park, or on privately-owned land where campsites are assigned and limited amenities may be provided – such as portable restrooms and running water. From a difficulty of operation standpoint, this is about as simple as it gets, and the barrier to entry is relatively low, but so is the return on investment.

Now, glampsites are something else entirely. The campers generally do not show up with tents and sleeping bags for a night spent under the stars. Instead, each campsite comes equipped with individual accommodations that more closely resemble tiny homes than tents. They might have a number of specific modifications like glass roofs for stargazing, mosquito netting enclosures around the outdoor spaces, and pre-built campfires where all one needs to do is strike a match. More substantial investment and levels of care are needed here, but they also provide much higher returns on investment.

Even as a writer, I never knew what a "yurt" was until a few weeks ago. As defined by Wikipedia, a yurt is a portable, round <u>tent</u> covered and <u>insulated</u> with skins or <u>felt</u>. Now, I know you might be getting caught up on the "skins and felt," but that is more of a traditional construction used back in ancient Mongolia. Today, yurts are readily available for purchase on Amazon and come in varying sizes and complexities, most of which are covered with canvas or other modern fabrics. But why did we just take this time to learn about yurts? Because the options for glamorizing them are endless.

A realtor we have worked with in the past recently constructed a yurt on the property behind her home. This is no ordinary yurt either. It is solar powered with incinerating toilets (yep, no sewer or septic – the waste is burned) and 100% organic bedding and toiletry products. It is marketed as an ecological destination of choice with hardly any carbon footprint. Is it going to be an ideal destination for most? Probably not, I know you won't catch me there. But, at over $300 per night and a booking calendar filled up months in advance, they have more than enough interest to make this a highly profitable idea.

RVs/Mobile Home Parks

These are nothing new, per se. Everywhere you look on social media or real estate-specific websites, there are purported gurus selling classes, webinars, and coaching on how to use their system to become the next millionaire mobile home park owner. The first step to deciding if this is a profitable investment opportunity is to realize the difference between an RV and a mobile home since the names are slightly misleading. RVs, or recreational vehicles, are completely mobile and can move from one location to another with relative ease. Mobile homes, however, are not nearly as mobile once set in place and connected to onsite utilities.

With that said, catering to the RV market leads to variable revenues as vehicles come and go. The mobile home parks offer slightly more stability when leasing plots of land to folks who own their own mobile home and just need a community to tie in with, but the real money in mobile home parks in this modern era of real estate is in owning the mobile home park and the homes within it. Even though a mobile home will not appreciate in value to the level a traditional home would, they are a relatively lower-cost alternative to purchase and will still yield rents on par with the local single-family or apartment housing market, making some of the return on investment numbers too attractive to ignore.

Much like the other alternate investment options, you have two options for getting into this market: buy an existing park or build your own. Needless to say, neither of those options are cheap, nor do they fit neatly into any one financing strategy. Buying an existing park will be the more costly option upfront, but at least you are stepping into an immediate cash flow situation and can approach an evaluation of the deal much like you would an individual rental property. Building a park from scratch will take time, patience, and resources amongst plenty of other intangible elements, such as connections and influence, to help push your plan forward to approval.

Financing options for mobile home or RV parks will also depend on whether you are buying existing or building from the ground up. Neither option will qualify for a traditional mortgage, but buying an existing business will have more options than building from the ground up. The nice thing about building though is that you not only get more control of the quality, but you also determine how quickly to expand. Stepping into an existing park with dozens or even hundreds of units can be daunting, especially without a solid management infrastructure. Building, so long as you own the land and put significant emphasis on planning, will allow you to build out in stages and maintain more control of the growth process.

Prefabricated Homes

Who doesn't love a good jigsaw puzzle or Lego block set? Sure, there is a big difference between assembling something without tools on your kitchen table and building a home you would feel comfortable enough to let your family inhabit, but the premise is the same. Prefabricated homes have existed for decades, but in a very different way than what is available today. No longer must a consumer settle for a limited number of styles or designs and rely on the manufacturer to assemble them.

With several breakout companies like Boxabl and Arched Cabins now revolutionizing the process of building and shipping homes, options have never been more customizable than they are now. This is a huge opportunity for more affordable home ownership options and for developers and investors to complete projects faster and more cost-effective than ever before. It is also likely the industry will continue to grow at a staggering rate as popularity takes root in consumer and investor markets.

Most of the strategies and disclaimers provided for tiny homes and container homes also apply here. The nice thing about working with prefabricated homes is that the industry is more familiar and comfortable with them, which should provide more options if you choose to go down this path. Also falling under this category could be modular homes, which are relatively the same with a slightly different construction process. Costs and availability will vary based on geography and current market demand, but these remain a lucrative alternative to building a brand new house from the ground up using traditional methods.

Commune Style Living

The word commune might make you think about cults or militias that have gone off the grid out in the middle of nowhere to get away from government oversight, but the word is more closely related to community, which is essentially what a commune is – a community of people who have come together for a common cause or purpose. Generally, all members of a commune share the same ideological beliefs and have common backgrounds and situations in life.

This style of living has become increasingly popular with the younger generations as the cost of living continues to rise. It takes the premise of having a roommate to share expenses with to the next level by organizing everyone living together to also share in the communal duties, such as shopping, cooking, and cleaning. For able-bodied elderly people who do not want to move in with their kids or assisted living facilities, this new trend offers a new option for living their golden years without sacrificing independence or quality of life. The opportunity to repurpose property for this style of living also provides new opportunities for investors and developers.

One of the two opportunities I see in this type of lifestyle shift pertains to quality of life issues and affording at-risk segments of the population more affordable options. Humans are a social species, and most would prefer to share in the company of others as opposed to languish in solitude. College students already embrace this strategy in the dorm or fraternity setup, only there they often do not have the luxury of choosing like-minded roommates. The same goes for the elderly who find themselves without a choice when well-intentioned family members ship them off to assisted living centers, where they also lose the power to choose. What a difference it could make if the young and impressionable along with the old and vulnerable had more control of their living situation.

The second opportunity lies in the potential access to more government (federal, state, or local) subsidies for offering this more affordable and accessible living model, which will hopefully incentivize more developers to take on projects like this. Numerous funding and tax abatement options already exist nationwide for the construction of affordable housing and developments geared to meet the Americans with Disabilities Act (ADA), and these communes are no different, so long as the project is presenting the needs and benefits to these protected classes without only focusing on the money the developer stands to make.

Whether you personally like any of these new trends or can't see yourself doing any of them, the potential is still there. Not everyone likes the same style of house, drives the same kind of car, or lives in the same part of the world. The beauty of change is that you don't have to adopt what you don't like, but you need to be aware of it. Real wealth can be created when you are able to see opportunities everyone else is looking past. Remember, many thought Steve Jobs was crazy for putting a camera in the iPhone, thinking no one would want that feature. Now, there is almost nothing we don't want on our phones.

If you or anyone you know is considering a career in real estate or looking to learn more about the myriad of investment opportunities you might never have heard of, reach out to chat with me today.

Resources

Please note these resources have all been designed to work in almost every scenario, with slight tweaking as needed. Everything in this section can be used by licensed real estate agents or private investors, even though certain areas will be more appealing to one group or the other. If you are a licensed agent, make sure to get permission from your broker or team leader before implementing any of these strategies, scripts, or tools to ensure adherence to whatever internal compliance guidelines they might have in place. Also, stay current on all local and federal laws as they pertain to cold calling (and texting) to avoid potential hefty fines.

Text Campaigns

Texting has become the primary mode of communication for people of all ages. While you will likely not close business in a text message, you will have the opportunity to start building a relationship in a casual, nonintrusive way. Estimates from sales marketing firms vary on the actual success rate of text messages, but most agree over 95% of all text messages are read by the recipient at some point, unlike voicemails that can go unlistened forever. Of that 95%, 90% are read within the first few minutes the message is sent. Texting is meant to be a tool to make your prospect aware of who you are, so when the time does come to make a phone call, they will likely recognize your number, and it will no longer be a "cold" call.

No matter what kind of outreach you are doing, do not forget how many touches you will need to make on average before finally finding someone interested in having a conversation. You may very well go 10 or more touches without ever getting a reply or only speaking to a voicemail. There will even be some people who still do not want to engage after the average 26+ touches. That is just the nature of the beast, and the quicker you learn to accept it and focus on the leads who are interested, the easier the process will be.

Let's look at a few different sequences we have successfully employed for landing listings on the license front and deals on the investor front. After the first three messages for each scenario, you can get creative with how you want to continue interacting with them. I find "happy holiday" text messages or handwritten cards break up the sales monotony nicely, but you can also forward interesting articles, provide updates on industry news, or check on their safety after a weather-related incident. The goal is to stay in touch and build a relationship until they have a need for your services.

The following sequences can and should be modified based on the prospect's response to your messages. Once they engage in a conversation, you will want to leverage their responses for future conversations so they feel like you are listening and genuinely care about what they have to say.

FSBO

Text #1:

> Hi (INSERT PROSPECT NAME),
>
> This is (INSERT YOUR NAME) with (INSERT COMPANY NAME). I just wanted to commend you on taking the first step in selling your home located at (INSERT PROPERTY ADDRESS)! In this market, you should be able to move fairly quickly. My team and I specialize in helping sellers find a new home anywhere in the country. We would love to find out more about where you want to go and how we can make the transition easier for you. Thank you!

Text #2 (7 days later):

> Hey (INSERT PROSPECT NAME),
>
> (INSERT YOUR NAME) with (INSERT COMPANY NAME) again. I hope all is moving along smoothly will the sale of your house. If you have any questions about the process, I would be happy to help answer them while helping you find your next place. Thank you!

Text #3 (7 days later):

> Hey (INSERT PROSPECT NAME),
>
> (INSERT YOUR NAME) with (INSERT COMPANY NAME) just circling back to see how everything is going. It looks like your home has been on the market for two weeks now, and most of our sellers are getting into contract sooner. Please let me know if there would be a good time for us to speak about your relocation plans. Thank you!

Off-Market

Text #1:

> Hello,
>
> My name is (INSERT YOUR NAME), and I am a private real estate investor in your area. I drove by your home at (INSERT ADDRESS), and it really caught my eye. I was just wondering if you had ever given any thought to selling it. I can close quickly with all cash and avoid using realtors, so you walk away with the most money. If you're not looking to sell but might know someone in the neighborhood who is, I would be happy to see if their house is a good fit as well. Thank you!

Text #2 (7 days later):

Hi again.

(INSERT YOUR NAME) here, just making sure you got my last message. I don't want to keep bothering you if you are not interested in selling, but if you are, I feel like we could get you a great deal and do all the legwork for you. Please reply either way, so we can stop texting you if there is no interest. Thank you!

Text #3 (7 days later):

Hey,

Sorry to be a pest, but I really do see potential in your home and would love to have a quick conversation about what the magic number would be in terms of a sales price. I will be back in your neighborhood next week and would be happy to stop by and introduce myself so you can put a face to the name. Thank you!

Distressed

Text #1:

Hello,

My name is (INSERT YOUR NAME), and I am (SPECIFY IF AGENT OR INVESTOR). I specialize in helping people who might be experiencing financial hardship stay in their home. I'm not sure if this applies to you or anyone you know, but if it does, I would love to have a conversation about our services. We do not charge anything for going to bat for you against the bank. Thank you!

Text #2 (7 days later):

Hey,

(INSERT YOUR NAME) here, just making sure you got my last message. I know not all the public data we have access to is always accurate, but recent filings indicate you might be behind on your mortgage payments. If this is not correct, please make sure you reach out to the local municipality or your mortgage company to remove the filing so your credit score does not suffer. If it is accurate, I would love to help you negotiate with the bank. As someone who has helped many owners avoid foreclosure, I understand just how difficult and emotional this can be. Thank you!

Text #3 (7 days later):

Hey,

(INSERT YOUR NAME) again. I don't want to keep texting you, as I am sure more people than you like are trying to separate you from our home. Please note that is not my objective. In the event a home does need to be sold, we fight to get our clients top dollar, but in most cases, we are able to convince the bank it is in their best interest to work with you. I will be back in your neighborhood next week and would be happy to stop by and introduce myself so you can put a face to the name. Thank you!

Analysis Tools

Cash Flow Calculator

CATEGORY	BUDGET	ACTUAL	% ACHIEVED	COMMENT
Income				
Unit 1				
Unit 2				
Unit 3				
Parking				
Storage				
Misc				
(=) GROSS RENT ROLL				
Expenses				
Mortgage				
Taxes				
Insurance				
Gas				
Electric				
Water				
Oil				
Trash				
Sewer				
HOA				

(=) TOTAL EXPENSES				
Profitability				
Gross Rent Roll				
(-) Vacancy rate (10%):				
(-) Maintenance (10%):				
(-) Total expenses:				
(=) NET CASH FLOW				

Flip Calculator

CATEGORY	BUDGET	ACTUAL	% ACHIEVED	COMMENT
Acquisition Costs				
Purchase Price				
Closing Costs				
Referral Fees				
Renovation Costs				
Roof				
Foundation				
Electrical				

HVAC				
Plumbing				
Bathrooms				
Kitchen				
Floors				
Sheetrock				
Paint/Trim				
Exterior				
Holding Costs				
Interest				
Taxes				
Insurance				
Landscaping				
Utilities				
Selling Costs				
Realtor				
Closing Costs				
Transfer Taxes				
Income Taxes				
Marketing				

Purchase Offers

Strongest Offer

TIME AWAY GROUP
MATTHEW HARMS - BROKER

PURCHASE OFFER

DATE:	September 1, 2023
PROPERTY:	123 Main St. Anytown, USA

BUYER:	Lavish Properties, LLC and/or assigns
ADDRESS:	1102 North St
CITY, STATE, ZIP:	Bronx, NY 10461

OFFER PRICE:	$215,000
TERMS:	All cash; 50% at contract signing
CONDITIONS:	None
INCLUSIONS:	None
CONTRACT:	ASAP
CLOSING:	30 days

BUYER ATTY:	Joe Lawyer
ADDRESS:	456 Broadway
CITY, STATE, ZIP:	New York, NY 10002
PHONE:	212-555-4567
EMAIL:	joe@lawyers.com

At first glance, this might seem identical to the next offer, but there are a few notable differences. First, the cash at closing is specific and far greater than the standard 10% most buyers will put down. It also waives all inclusions, meaning they do not care if the mechanical systems and appliances work. It also does not ask for the unit to be delivered vacant, which is a huge plus.

Middle Offer

TIME AWAY GROUP
MATTHEW HARMS - BROKER

PURCHASE OFFER

DATE:	September 1, 2023
PROPERTY:	123 Main St. Anytown, USA

BUYER:	John Smith
ADDRESS:	1102 North St
CITY, STATE, ZIP:	Bronx, NY 10461

OFFER PRICE:	$265,000
TERMS:	All cash
CONDITIONS:	Delivered vacant
INCLUSIONS:	All appliances and mechanical systems
CONTRACT:	ASAP
CLOSING:	30 days

BUYER ATTY:	Joe Lawyer
ADDRESS:	456 Broadway
CITY, STATE, ZIP:	New York, NY 10002
PHONE:	212-555-4567
EMAIL:	joe@lawyers.com

While still an all-cash offer, this buyer does not specify how much will be given at contract signing. It also specifically requests the home be delivered vacant with all mechanical systems and appliances in working order.

Get Real!

Weakest Offer

TIME AWAY GROUP
MATTHEW HARMS - BROKER

PURCHASE OFFER

DATE:	September 1, 2023
PROPERTY:	123 Main St. Anytown, USA

BUYER:	John Smith
ADDRESS:	1102 North St
CITY, STATE, ZIP:	Bronx, NY 10461

OFFER PRICE:	$265,000
TERMS:	10% down at contract signing, 10% at closing, 80% conventional mortgage
CONDITIONS:	Inspection, Mortgage Approval
INCLUSIONS:	All appliances, mechanical systems, and outdoor furniture
CONTRACT:	1 week
CLOSING:	On or about 11/1/2023

BUYER ATTY:	Joe Lawyer
ADDRESS:	456 Broadway
CITY, STATE, ZIP:	New York, NY 10002
PHONE:	212-555-4567
EMAIL:	joe@lawyers.com

The only thing this offer has going for it is the higher purchase price. While $50K, or 25% more than the other offers, might sound attractive, the process will be longer and more cumbersome with plenty of places along the way for the deal to fall apart.

Templates

Lender Tracker

Lender	Program	Rate	LTV	Points	Credit	Fees	Full Doc
ABC Bank & Trust	Fix & Flip	6.95%+	90%	2	660+	$1,495	No
Local Community Bank	Purchase	5.25%+	80%	0	720+	$595	Yes
Jones Equity Partners	Purchase	9%+	75%	3	590+	$2,600	No
Ocean State Associates	Refinance	7%+	60%	0	660+	$0	Yes
Bankers United	Construction	10%+	65%	3	725+	$2,600	Yes

Buyer's Wishlist

PROPERTY SEARCH WISHLIST

Bedrooms   —————————

Bathrooms   —————————

Zip Codes   —————————

Ideal Price   —————————

Time Frame   —————————

Style	**Land**	**Condition**
☐ Ranch	☐ > .25 acres	☐ Fully Remodeled
☐ Split Level	☐ > .5 acres	☐ Needs some work
☐ Tudor	☐ > 1 acre	☐ Gut Rehab
☐ Colonial	☐ > 3 acres	
☐ Victorian	☐ 5 acres +	
☐ Cape Cod		
☐ Modern		
☐ Other —————		

Basement	**Attic**	**Pool**	**Garage**
☐ Must Have	☐ Must Have	☐ Must Have	☐ Must Have
☐ Nice to Have	☐ Nice to Have	☐ Nice to Have	☐ Nice to Have
☐ Don't Want	☐ Don't Want	☐ Don't Want	☐ Don't Want

Driveway	**Fireplace**	**Backyard**
☐ Must Have	☐ Must Have	☐ Must Have
☐ Nice to Have	☐ Nice to Have	☐ Nice to Have
☐ Don't Want	☐ Don't Want	☐ Don't Want

Closing Timeline

1. INSPECTION REPORT

Provided in approx. 48 hours after the inspection. Inspector will point out anything of major concern the day of so. Not necessary to wait for the formal report before proceeding.

2. CONTRACTS

Seller's attorney will send contracts to your attorney shortly after inspection is complete and satisfactory. Your attorney will review with you, get signatures, and coordinate the downpayment. In non-attorney states, the realtors will guide the process along the same time frames.

3. BANK

Once both parties have signed contracts, we can send to your banks, and they will begin the underwriting process, which includes ordering an appraisal.

4. APPRAISAL

Can take up to 3 weeks from the time the bank has fully executed contracts. After the appraisal is completed, it can take up to 3 weeks for the report to be submitted and reviewed by the bank.

5. TITLE REPORT

This is ordered around the same time as the appraisal and is done to make sure there are no liens or other issues with the property.

6. CLOSING

Anywhere between 45-75 days from when the contract was signed depending on the speed of the lender, appraiser, and title report, which can all take time in their own right.

Seller's Checklist

SELLER'S CHECKLIST

☐ **Warranties**   ☐ **Service Records**

☐ Roof   ☐ Boiler

☐ Boiler   ☐ Drain

☐ Central Air   ☐ Chimney

☐ Water Heater   ☐ Ducts

☐ Appliances

☐ **Curb Appeal**   ☐ **Painting**

☐ Manicured Lawn   ☐ **Inspection**

☐ Clean Siding   ☐ **Locate a New Home**

☐ Remove Trash   ☐ **Permits & Certificate of Occupancy**

Screen Potential Realtors

How many homes have you sold in this neighborhood?

_____

_____

How many listings do you currently have?

_____

_____

What makes you different from other agents?

_____

_____

What will you do for me I could not do myself?

_____

_____

Reading

- *The Ultimate Self-Directed IRA* by Jeff Astor

- *Tax Liens and Deeds Investment* by Graham Smith

Glossary

Appraisal Management Company (AMC): an independent entity through which mortgage lenders order residential real estate valuation services for properties they are considering extending loans to homebuyers on. AMCs are used to ensure mortgage lenders are not giving all their loans to select appraisers, thus keeping the process fairer and more transparent.

Business Line of Credit (BLOC): a revolving line of credit, similar to a credit card, issued by a bank to a business entity. They generally have a set credit limit, variable interest rate, and renewal period. The bank may or may not ask the owner of the business to personally guarantee the line.

Capitalization rate: a real estate valuation measure used to compare different real estate investments, generally calculated as the ratio between the net annual rental income produced by a real estate asset to its current market value.

Certificate of Occupancy (CO): a document issued by a local government agency or building department certifying a building's compliance with applicable building codes and other laws, indicating it to be in a condition suitable for occupancy.

Comparative Market Analysis (CMA): a document generally created by a licensed real estate professional that offers insight into the estimated value of a property by comparing sales data from similar property types and sizes in a certain geographic proximity, which has sold in the last six months.

Debt-to-Income (DTI): the percentage of your gross monthly income that is used to pay your monthly debt and determines your borrowing risk.

Emergency Rental Assistance Program (ERAP): designed to provide significant economic relief to help low and moderate-income households at risk of experiencing homelessness or housing instability by providing rental arrears, temporary rental assistance, and utility arrears assistance, with guidelines varying from state to state and county to county.

Fair Market Rent (FMR): the monthly amount of rent a property type is likely to receive in a particular area. The amount is determined by how much renters are able and willing to pay in your area, and the best indicator is what other landlords are charging their tenants for similar properties.

Fair Market Value (FMV): is the price a product would sell for on the open market, assuming both buyer and seller are reasonably knowledgeable about the asset, behaving in their own best interests, free of undue pressure, and given a reasonable time period for completing the transaction.

Federal Emergency Management Agency (FEMA): an agency within the U.S. Department of Homeland Security charged with responding to presidentially-declared disasters as well as administering the National Flood Insurance Program.

Federal Home Administration loan (FHA): a type of mortgage insured by the Federal Housing Administration (FHA). While the government insures these loans, they're underwritten and funded by third-party mortgage lenders approved by the FHA and come with a lower minimum credit score and down payment requirement than other loan options.

For Sale By Owner (FSBO): A property listed for sale directly by the homeowner or legal custodian without the assistance of a licensed real estate professional, saving the seller money on commission payouts but increasing the amount of work they will need to do themselves.

Home Equity Line of Credit (HELOC): a revolving type of secured loan in which the lender agrees to lend a maximum amount within an agreed period, where the collateral is the borrower's property, with specified interest rates and repayment terms.

Homeowners Association (HOA): an organization in a subdivision, planned community, or condominium building that makes and enforces rules for the properties and residents. Those who purchase property within an HOA's jurisdiction automatically become members and are required to pay dues, which are known as HOA fees.

Margin loan: allows you to borrow against the value of securities you already own. It's an interest-bearing loan that can be used to gain access to funds for a variety of reasons that cover both investment and non-investment needs.

Multiple Listing Service (MLS): private databases that are created, maintained, and paid for by real estate professionals to help their clients buy and sell property. In most cases, access to information from MLS listings is provided to the public free-of-charge by participating brokers. Data that is not publicly accessible includes information that would endanger sellers' privacy or safety, such as seller contact information and times the home is vacant for showings.

Limited Liability Company (LLC): the United States-specific form of a private limited company. It is a business structure that can combine the pass-through taxation of a partnership or sole proprietorship with the limited liability of a corporation.

Loan-to-Value (LTV): a financial term used by lenders to express the ratio of a loan to the value of an asset purchased. In real estate, the term is commonly used by banks and building societies to represent the ratio of the first mortgage line as a percentage of the total appraised value of real property.

Private equity (PE): capital investments made into not publicly traded companies by firms comprised of accredited investors or high-net-worth individuals.

Private Mortgage Insurance (PMI): a type of mortgage insurance you might be required to buy if you take out a conventional loan with a down payment of less than 20 percent of the purchase price, for the purpose of protecting the lender in the event you default on the loan.

Purchase money mortgage: a mortgage issued to the borrower by the seller of a home as part of the purchase transaction. Also known as a seller or owner financing, this is usually done in situations where the buyer cannot qualify for a mortgage through traditional lending channels.

Rent roll: the gross amount of rental income derived from an investment property or portfolio of properties that can be expressed in either monthly or annual figures.

Self-directed IRA: a type of individual retirement account that gives you more control and flexibility over the investments in the account. You can own a broader range of assets that go beyond traditional options like stocks, bonds, and funds with the same tax advantages and rules as a conventional IRA.

Seller's concession: closing costs the seller pays to help the buyer by reducing the amount of cash they need to close. Also called seller assists or seller contributions.

Veterans Administration loans (VA): a mortgage loan available through a program established by the U.S. Department of Veterans Affairs (VA) (previously the Veterans Administration). With VA loans, veterans, service members, and their surviving spouses can purchase homes with little to no down payment and no private mortgage insurance and generally get a competitive interest rate.

Made in the USA
Middletown, DE
15 October 2023

40722999R00126